Teachers Under Pressure

Teachers Under Pressure

Maurice Galton and John MacBeath

Los Angeles • London • New Delhi • Singapore

© Maurice Galton and John MacBeath 2008

Co publication with the NUT

First published 2008

SAGE Publications Ltd
1 Oliver's Yard
55 City Road
London EC1Y 1SP

SAGE Publications Inc.
2455 Teller Road
Thousand Oaks, California 91320

SAGE Publications India Pvt Ltd
B 1/I 1 Mohan Cooperative Industrial Area
Mathura Road
New Delhi 110 044

SAGE Publications Asia-Pacific Pte Ltd
33 Pekin Street #02-01
Far East Square
Singapore 048763

Library of Congress Control Number: 2007937687

British Library Cataloguing in Publication data

A catalogue record for this book is available from
the British Library

ISBN 978-1-84787-321-7
ISBN 978-1-84787-322-4 (pbk)

Typeset by CEPHA Imaging Pvt. Ltd., Bangalore, India
Printed in Great Britain by The Cromwell Press Ltd, Trowbridge, Wiltshire
Printed on paper from sustainable resources

Contents

About the authors   vi
Acknowledgements   vii

Introduction   1

Chapter 1:   Teaching is not what it used to be   4

Chapter 2:   Balancing the workload equation: A continuing story   13

Chapter 3:   A life in teaching: The primary teacher's experience?   23

Chapter 4:   Remodelling the primary teaching workforce   32

Chapter 5:   A life in secondary teaching   43

Chapter 6:   The inclusion enigma: The policy context   57

Chapter 7:   The inclusion enigma findings and implications of
             the study   67

Chapter 8:   Workload agreements and the rise of the teaching assistant   81

Chapter 9:   It's the same the whole world over: What happens in
             other countries?   93

Chapter 10: Remodelling: Structures or mindset?   104

References   117
Index   124

About the authors

Maurice Galton

Professor Maurice Galton is a former Dean of Education at Leicester University. He was appointed Associate Director of Research at Homerton College, Cambridge in 1999 and now works in the Faculty of Education. He is best known for his work on teaching and learning in the primary school, including the ORACLE project and for the study of transfer from primary to secondary school. His latest book, *Learning and Teaching in the Primary School* is also published by Sage. Professor Galton is currently engaged in a study of the pedagogy of artists who work in UK schools and he also holds consultancies with the Hong Kong Education Department where he is evaluating the effect of reducing class size in primary schools.

John MacBeath

Professor John MacBeath OBE, is Chair of Educational Leadership at the Faculty of Education at the University of Cambridge and Director of Leadership for Learning: the Cambridge Network. His research and consultancy brings together work with schools and with policy makers in Britain as well as internationally. He has worked in a consultancy capacity with the OECD, UNESCO and the European Commission and currently advises policy makers in Hong Kong on school self evaluation and inspection. For a decade he has worked closely with the National Union of Teachers and since 2002 has conducted four studies for the NUT with his Cambridge colleague Maurice Galton. He is currently President of the International Congress and School Improvement.

Acknowledgements

We would like to thank Sally Roach and Katie O' Donovan for their support and patience in keeping us organised and in preparation of the text. Thanks too to Jude Bowen of Sage for having faith in the book from the outset and helping it come to fruition. To the schools who participated a particular thank you for giving us your time not only once but equally welcoming on our second visits. Finally, a deep vote of thanks to the NUT who made all of this possible through the excellent offices of John Bangs and the late Steve Sinnott.

Maurice Galton and John MacBeath

Introduction

What has been the impact of various policy initiatives on the working lives of teachers over the last two decades? Has the government's remodelling agenda made a life in teaching easier and more fulfilling, as it was intended to do; and if not what is preventing the desired improvements from taking place? These are the central themes which this book seeks to address.

The research on which the book is based has been carried out over a five-year period. It began with an exploration of teacher's lives in primary schools in 2002 prompted in part by a report to government by PricewaterhouseCoopers in 2001, suggesting that the tasks teachers performed could be divided into 'low'- and 'high'-level activities, recommending that the former could either be done by less well-qualified staff or automated using the latest information technology. Following our first study in primary schools we explored these issues in a secondary context, with a third study focusing on inclusive policies, which had proved such a recurring theme in the two prior studies. Since the School Workforce Agreement was also being implemented over the same period, we returned to some of the schools we had visited earlier to determine what changes had taken place and to assess their impact on teachers' work-life balance.

Chapter One considers the effects of 'intensification', the resultant loss of autonomy and a sense of no longer being in control of how and what one teaches. Chapter Two takes a historical perspective, charting ways in which policy initiatives over the last two decades have added to the pressures in the workplace. The following five chapters then further explore the impact of policy changes on teachers' lives, with particular focus on the remodelling process and special needs provision. Chapter Eight deals with the ever expanding role of the teaching assistants who, under remodelling, have assumed many of the tasks formally thought to be the sole prerogative of qualified teachers.

Chapter Nine then takes on an international perspective, charting common themes in four countries (Canada, Hong Kong, New Zealand and Australia). 'Intensification' is a prevailing concern, leaving many teachers with the feeling that time-consuming initiatives are designed to control performance rather than benefit pupils' educational development. In brief, teachers feel they are no longer trusted to teach effectively. This is a significant finding since early research on 'teacher burnout' demonstrated that coping with the high stress levels was possible, provided teachers felt that they retained a high degree of autonomy in deciding what and how to teach. In the final chapter, therefore we try to take a positive stance and to suggest ways in which the stress caused by these 'universal problems' might be eliminated, or at best reduced.

However, this book is more than an account of the working conditions of teachers. Across the globe research indicates that the lives of teachers are more stressful and that the balance between their personal lives and work is often unacceptable to their families and close friends. Yet this situation does not appear amenable to the more straightforward explanations often put forward to account for this state of affairs. In the UK, for example, teachers claim that the pressure emanates from the centralised reforms which are accompanied by excessive bureaucratic procedures, but in Australia, where central government has little control over education policy teachers also complain of similar pressures. Again in Hong Kong, workloads are in excess of those reported elsewhere but the aim of government reform has been to reduce central control and give more freedom to schools.

It would seem likely, therefore, that across the globe there exist a variety of explanations to account for the present circumstances in teaching so that in the final analysis, insofar as there are common solutions, these need to concentrate on what teachers, schools and those who work with them and are concerned for their welfare can do to make schools better places for teachers and for those whose future they vouchsafe.

We have to acknowledge the help of several persons and organisations in writing this book. First, our thanks go to Charlotte Page and Susan Steward who carried out many of the case studies and surveys and to Andrea MacBeath who also helped with the study of inclusion. Second, thanks go to Sally Roach and Katie O' Donovan who provided organisational and clerical support. Third, our thanks to Jude Bowen at Sage who had faith in this book from the beginning and helped to steer its course. Finally, our thanks go to the National Union of Teachers (NUT) who sponsored our research and to their Assistant Secretary, John Bangs, in particular, who was able to guide us through the mass of government legislation without ever attempting to impinge on our academic freedom in matters of interpretation.

Our final thanks go to the teachers who gave up their time to answer our questions. Without them there would be no book. We trust that there was some benefit in being able to talk to an 'outsider' who had some sympathetic understanding of their problems. It is our hope that this book helps to reduce this dissonance by widening the debate about work-life balance beyond mere managerial solutions.

Maurice Galton
John MacBeath

1

Teaching Is Not What It Used to Be

In this first chapter we identify some of the factors that have impacted on teachers' working lives in recent years both in the UK and elsewhere. While in a more challenging world the teaching impulse has endured, teachers are leaving the profession 'in unprecedented numbers' as the OECD (Organisation for Economic Cooperation and Development) claims. This, our evidence suggests, is because successive government reforms have succeeded in progressively draining off the enthusiasm and commitment for teaching, so that the greatest professional source of satisfaction – seeing children learn – is progressively undermined by tables, targets and the tyranny of testing.

The end of a golden age?

Teaching is not what it used to be. The brave new world in which schools find themselves is not what it used to be and the lives of children are no longer as innocent as they once were. Yet the teaching impulse has not changed commensurately. Teaching may be tougher, more challenging, requiring greater resilience and tolerance, but the satisfaction derived from watching children learn and grow is still its primary reward. Teachers enter the profession for a variety of motives, sometimes by default, sometimes through a love of their subject, sometimes through a desire to work with children, but it is only when teachers get their first taste of the Eureka moment that teaching becomes an addictive vocation. The teacher of the year 2007, receiving his award from

Lord Putnam, confessed to entering teaching in the first place simply to prolong his time at University by taking the PGCE post-graduate teaching qualification (Kingston, 2007). However, once inside the classroom and recognising the awesome responsibility as a powerful agent for change he admitted to being hooked for life.

Yet, teaching is not what it used to be. Not because the impulse to teach has diminished but because teachers now have to deal with pressures qualitatively different than ever before. Since the invention of schooling teachers have had to cope with indisciplined and troubled children and put up with unreasonable demands from government bodies, but the scale, complexity and intensity of pressures on them in the postmodern world are unprecedented.

It may be argued that today's teachers are less isolated in their classrooms, that they receive more support from their colleagues and senior leaders, that they are less reluctant to share their problems and admit to their failings, yet this is also a double-edged sword. Classrooms are now more transparent and the nature of teaching and learning are open to almost continuous scrutiny. A variety of stakeholders – local authorities, School Improvement Partners, Ofsted inspectors, parents and pupils are encouraged to hold teachers to account for the 'delivery' of the curriculum and the perpetual raising of standards. Accountability goes in hand in hand with 'perverse indicators' (O'Neill, 2002), and performance management, performance tables and per-formance testing tell a story of a system which seems to unable to learn from the mistakes of the past. There is worrying conformation for this from the ongoing Primary Review (2007) whose early findings reveal 'a pervasive anxiety about specific aspects of recent educational policy' and cast doubt on the government's view that the testing regime raises standards. It also begins to paint a picture of the world in which childhood ends too prema-turely and children arrive at the school gates knowing too much and not enough.

Teaching has had to rise to the challenge of a world in which the pace, nature and contexts of learning have been radically transformed. Teachers entering the profession today may expect classrooms to be like the ones they attended but although a teaching space may look surprisingly similar on the surface, the quality and dynamics of what happens there are not what they used to be. While the curriculum may have a reassuring familiarity, its value is now measured less in intrinsic terms than as a proxy for a school's or a teacher's effectiveness. 'Delivery', a word in common usage borrowed from industry and misapplied in a classroom context, places the teacher as intermediary between a body of required knowledge and pupil performance, stripping him or her of the creative and interpretive role that they could play given a degree of latitude, creative diversion and a genuine sense of ownership.

The contemporary world is one in which young people are less and less inclined to be simply at the receiving end of a delivered curriculum. They are growing up faster and with alternative attractions more engaging than what their schools have to offer. Yet, for governments, the solution seems to lie in greater containment, stricter testing regimes and ever-increasing pressure on teachers to prove themselves, against benchmarks, 'best practice' and mandated criteria of effectiveness. Teachers are, suggests Day (2000), confused by the loose-tight paradox of local decision-making responsibilities alongside increased public scrutiny and external accountability, leading to what has been described as 'intensification'. It is captured well in the following extract from a case study of a New York City school.

> Nine and a half hour days, class on Saturday, school during the summer and two hours of homework each night are non-negotiable... "If you're off the bus you're working," says Feinberg... "Each morning students receive a worksheet of maths, logic and word problems for them to solve in the free minutes that appear during the day."

> Teachers carry cell phones with toll free numbers and are on call 24 hours a day to answer any concerns their students might have. "Ten calls a night may sound like a drag", says Feinberg, "but everyone goes to bed ready for the next school day." (Principal Michael Feinberg, in Carter, 2001:95)

The question it raises is one of sustainability. 'Burnout' is a term that has now entered the teaching lexicon as teachers find that they cannot sustain the intensity of investment in teaching and in meeting the needs of their students. For many young people, engaging with the curriculum may come low down in the hierarchy of needs. For many teachers, teaching one's subject may also assume a lower priority than that of simply finding some emotional stability with troubled young people and establishing some common ground on which to communicate.

This is not a purely British or North American phenomenon. It is equally familiar in Australia, New Zealand, Singapore, Hong Kong and Japan, for example. Shimahara (2003:3) characterises Japanese schools as experiencing 'the troubled relationship between the children who are the main actors in the educational process and the system itself'. He locates it in systemic factors.

> Intensification refers to the loss of autonomy, caused by prescribed programs, mandated curricula, step-by-step methods of instruction combined with pressure to respond to various innovations and diversification of students' academic and social needs.

However, as Shimahara goes on to discuss, those common global forces play out differently in different cultural contexts. In Japan intensification is seen as coming from within, teachers accepting their lot, what is termed *shukumei*, a situation not be challenged. Shimahara quotes a teacher:

> In our work there is neither beginning nor end because it just continues. It would be best to complete everything at school but it is impossible. I have to bring my work home and spend one or two hours on it every day. (p. 23)

Even a decade ago, as revealed in a study by Fujita (1997), it was found that the majority of Japanese teachers spent at least ten hours in school every day, middle school teachers 11–12 hours, as many as half staying until 8 p.m.

There is a similar stoicism in Hong Kong schools (MacBeath and Clark, 2005) where a powerful normative culture discourages teachers from departing from the mainstream of practice. While in these cultures intensification may be described as 'self imposed' it has to be understood as a collective response, deriving from a sense of professional duty.

While in Western cultures there is greater tendency to make one's complaints heard, it is claimed, at least in the US context, 'that teachers have operated for so long under this cultural dysfunction that they regulate themselves with their own bureaucratic chains (Troen and Coles, 2004). The authors refer to Foucault's Panopticon, the all-seeing eye, inducing a state of conscious and constant surveillance which becomes permanent in its effects. In the English context too, in which teachers are more inclined to voice their discontent, we found a great deal of outspoken complaint about policy, pressure and deprofessionalisation, yet at the same time a dutiful compliance to the inevitability of the situation (Galton and MacBeath, 2002; MacBeath and Galton, 2004). Referring to stress in range of occupations, including teaching, Tennant (2001) writes:

> The problem of assessing what may be acceptable or unacceptable stress is further confused by virtue of the fact that increasing responsibilities and hours worked are becoming more common in the workplace and thus seem 'normative'. (p. 702)

While living with intensification often expresses itself simply in resentful resignation, it also results in resignation in a more fundamental sense, in other words, withdrawal from a situation seen as no longer tenable. As various research studies show internationally, teachers are leaving the profession in unprecedented numbers. An OECD Education Policy Analysis in 2001 warned of a 'meltdown scenario' caused by a growing teacher exodus from the profession. It reported widespread public dissatisfaction with the state of education in the face of a deep teacher-recruitment crisis and a growing sense of declining standards, especially in the worst affected areas. A year later a report by the General Teaching Council in Wales (GTCW, 2002) described the fulfillment of that forecast with one in ten teaching posts remaining unfilled. Its Chief Executive claimed 'Clearly heads don't believe they have enough choice of applicants to make the appointments they want... In some cases, they had no choices at all.'

Often the teacher exodus occurs after a short period in post. Ingersoll (2003) describes this as the 'revolving door syndrome'. Teaching is a profession that loses new recruits very early and schools are, he says, suffering from lack of autonomy and flexibility in addressing pedagogical issues creatively. This resonates with findings from an Australian study (Wilhelm *et al.*, 2000) that has been following a cohort of teachers since 1978. They found that teachers who left did so within the first five years of teaching. If a school provided mechanisms for the protection of academic freedom and for voicing opposition where there was disagreement with school policies, teachers would be less likely to exit. If, however, there were few mechanisms for the collective or individual expression of disagreement and few protections for those who challenged state or school or policies, dissenting teachers were more likely to exit.

The consequent danger is that by draining off dissent, the vitality, scope and diversity of the organisation is potentially diminished. There is a substantive body of evidence to suggest that compliance stifles creativity and initiative and that consensus can close down creative alternatives (Surowiecki, 2004).

In the US context, Susan Moore Johnson (2004) writes that teaching is no longer a career for life, no longer for first career entrants prepared for the job in traditional ways, operating privately and autonomously in their own classrooms. Between 24 and 40 per cent of teachers in her study, depending on the state or city of their recruitment, were mid-career entrants. Those who came from industry looked for opportunities to work in teams and to have expanded influence. The 'hole in the bucket' inflow and outflow of staff is, she argues, an expression of a shifting socio-economic situation that is unlikely to be attenuated without a quality of leadership willing to attend to the changing expectations that teachers bring with them – in Andy Hargreaves (2005) words 'reading the tea leaves'.

The combination of rapid change and timidity of response by policy makers calls for a quality of leadership, able to 'resist the juggernaut' (Frost, 2005), strong enough to maintain an educational vision with moral integrity and intellectual subversion. Ironically, the recruitment and retention 'crisis' impacts most acutely on school leadership.

Williams' (2001) Canadian study of recruitment to principalship listed 22 'dissatisfiers', many of which find an echo in other national studies. While the reference here is to principalship/headship these same dissatisfiers appear to apply at all levels within the teaching profession.

Stress

Stress is one of the strongest recurring themes in the literature, its source lying in constant change and the changing nature of the job. In Canada, Leithwood (www.oise.utoronto.ca/orbit/school_leader) reported a rise in stress levels 'considerably exaggerated over the past two years in Ontario as a consequence of the speed with which policy changes have been introduced'. Decentralisation and the competitive nature of a market economy bring with them a need to work harder, more demanding hours and in face of progressively higher stakes. Much of the stress is explained in terms of principals/head teachers having more responsibilities than power (Thomson *et al.*, 2003), carrying on their own shoulders responsibility for the success or failure of their schools, and delivering success, in the currency of test scores within a prescribed period and in a turbulent socio-economic context, where few things stand still enough to be measured.

Stress may be just as acute in the case of teachers. As it is highly correlated with the amount of control one has over decision-making (Martin, 1997), its effects may be felt most profoundly among staff who see themselves caught between a highly prescriptive agenda and a room full of young people who need to be coerced and cajoled into engaging with the matter at hand. Stress is not unique to teaching. It is experienced among a wide range of professions but there is a form of stress for many classroom teachers that teachers describe as distinctive, debilitating and demoralising. This was a continuous theme in our own tripartite studies of primary, secondary and special schools which provide the content for this book.

The rigid structure of the National Curriculum, particularly the pressure to meet curriculum targets, the excessive levels of testing (over a third of KS2 teachers tested mathematics once a week) and the preparations required for Ofsted inspections were the particular source of frustration. Not only did these activities generate considerable amounts of paperwork which could not be undertaken by unqualified staff, but more importantly called into question the teacher's professional competence in managing pupils' learning. Not feeling in control of their work was a major cause of teacher stress.

These issues were compounded for teachers who had to deal with 'difficult and needy' children in the absence of specialist care and expertise.

> I am luckier in some ways than my secondary colleagues. I don't have homework to mark or lessons to prepare in the same way. My stress is different. It is dealing with some of the very most difficult and needy of children. Their needs are such that they can't be met in a school without the very specialist care and support they need. Many of the problems I deal with are home problems. Calling parents, what's gone well, what's not gone well, keeping in touch with staff to make sure not just that the pupils are all right but that staff are coping. Nothing is predictable. (SENCO, secondary school)

Accountability and bureaucracy

Feelings of stress and workload are closely related to issues of accountability and bureaucracy. Portin (2004) describes the principalship in the US as 'a powerless position mired in bureaucracy'. Half a decade earlier, in the UK context, accountability and attendant bureaucracy were identified in Draper and McMichael's 2000 study as significant disincentives to applying for headship. Heads and teachers alike acknowledged the importance of accountability but excessive form filling and paperwork combined with a constant pressure to justify one's actions led to a feeling of not being in control of one's own destiny. Giving testimony to the Parliamentary Select Committee Peter Mortimore said 'the responsibilities are pretty daunting and chances are you are going to be blamed and shamed for things which perhaps are out of your control'

(Parliamentary Report, Item 167). 'Blame and shame' is also cited as a cause of principal demotivation in New Zealand (Livingstone, 1999), while in the US the added threat of litigation compounded the problems. Accountability has acquired negative connotations, researchers conclude, not only because it is highly demanding but because it is often directed at the wrong things.

In Hong Kong, the introduction of the School Development and Accountability policy saw an immediate rise in the 'paper chase' (MacBeath and Clark, 2005) with principals and teachers alike expressing anxiety over the accountability aspect of the new policy, resulting in the Education and Manpower Bureau reducing documentation, numbers and length of meetings, public reporting of results and initiating a more teacher friendly form of external review.

In our three English studies, teachers often spoke with bitter feeling about the combination of bureaucratic demands and external accountability that were driving them out of teaching.

> I have lived/taught through a period where we were respected as professionals and if asked we would do whatever was requested. Now heavy accountability has replaced this. I have excellent examination results, the pupils love my lessons and write to me after leaving describing what they ended up doing and thank me but I now hate the job and am considering leaving for a career in entomology. (Science teacher, 21 years' experience)

Personal and domestic concerns

Many of those who go into teaching do not see themselves as aspiring to headship. Commentators (Tucker and Codding, 2002) describe the challenges of 'crossing the professional border' into school leadership and cite anxiety, and information perplexity as explaining reluctance to put oneself forward. For many teachers it would seem that the balance between classroom teaching and family life is threatened by the 'burden of headship'. Researchers in both UK (James and Whiting, 1998) and in Australia (d'Arbon et al., 2001) suggest that many staff are content to remain as classroom teachers because principalship implies not only longer hours but can also involve travel away from the home base and they do not want to be separated from children. 'Trailing the spouse', sometimes involving dislocation of family and home or temporary separation, are cited as further disincentives. The decision to apply for headship positions is for many prospective school leaders determined ultimately by their reflection 'on the balance of lifestyle' and the weighing up of incentives and disincentives of the job, conclude James and Whiting (1998).

In our own three studies, head teachers and teachers referred constantly to the tensions between their home and professional lives. We found teachers not only working longer hours but taking home an increasingly large amount of marking and preparation work. One primary school teacher wrote on her questionnaire: 'It took such a huge and constant strain on our marriage. I am now divorced.'

Societal factors

At a time when many people view schools as one of the few intact social organisations, students arrive with very different attitudes, motivations and needs than their counterparts of three or four decades ago (Normore, 2004). We are, writes Normore, living in a society where social relationships, parenting and attitudes of young people are experiencing dramatic and often unforeseen changes. The increasing diversity of the student population, multiplicity of language and ethnic backgrounds, short-term refugeeism, the casualties of war, transience of the student body, concentrations of poverty in inner cities and depopulated rural areas, all bring their own, often formidable, challenges. Problems such as drug abuse, intimidation and violence create dilemmas which are beyond the power of schools to resolve but have repercussions within the school walls. For schools, particularly in areas of severe deprivation, there is an increase in the incidence of confrontation and conflict, heightening the need for mediation and intervention and negotiation with parents and other social agencies. Head teachers in urban schools, it was found (MacBeath *et al.*, 2006) spend proportionately more time outside their school than their counterparts in other locations. A 2004 World Bank report (Moreno, 2004) on schools in the Ukraine and Bulgaria found that school leaders spent 70 per cent of their time on raising finance, and the remaining 30 per cent on conflict resolution.

Dealing with conflict in the many forms in which it is expressed proves to be one of the factors which wears down school staff through a slow and unrelenting process of attrition. Discipline problems are often deeply rooted and not amenable to a quick fix. As teachers are themselves under so much pressure issues are left unresolved, and problems then resurface in other places. Intensification fuels a climate in which conflict is endemic. Discipline issues overflow the classroom and infect the teacher culture. Perhaps the clearest of all findings from our three studies were the troublesome and pervasive repercussions of disruption to lessons. In our secondary study (2004), we asked teachers to choose the five issues that they regarded as most serious and to rank them in order. Topping the list, and chosen by 75 per cent of our sample, was pupil behaviour. This was a mounting problem in which teachers could no longer reach for effective sanctions.

> It's the abuse you get really. I don't think anyone else, like when you're with friends and no one else would go to work in an office and be told to f.. off and be expected to put up with it. It's what really drags you down. But I do like working in this school. The pupils can be funny and challenging at times and I do enjoy that but ... it's disheartening sometimes. (Head of History, 4 years' experience)

In respect of children with complex and profound learning difficulties teachers were quick to recognise that this was not a disciplinary issue but one beyond their understanding or control. Young people who were unable to control their own behaviour could have a hugely disruptive effect on learning and have a ripple effect which gave license to others to exploit the unsettled ethos of the classroom.

Salary

Research into dissatisfiers for head teachers/principals salary has been frequently cited as an issue, with comparison made between levels of responsibility of school leadership with leadership in other occupations. In Australia, 'disaffection with principals' salary was a strong deterrent to teachers applying for promotion (d'Arbon *et al.*, 2001). Comparisons were made with similar positions of responsibility in industry or commerce 'where the management of human and material resources was seen as equivalent but not as highly recompensed' (d' Arbon *et al.*, 2001:12). Principals, it was claimed, also earn less per hour than their staff as they work 30 per cent longer hours in a week.

Salary also figures as an issue with teachers, although as with heads, is lower down the priority list because, as one teacher in our secondary study said, 'Despite it all, teaching is in the genes' and it is not the money that motivates nor the career prospects, but the intrinsic satisfaction from seeing young people learn and grow.

Workload

Topping the poll in almost every survey of lives teachers' professional lives is the issue of workload. In many different countries this is seen as the leading explanatory factor for teacher stress, dissatisfaction and burnout, leading ultimately to the exit door. As we report in Chapters 4 and 5 it is exacerbated by disciplinary issues, and (in Chapters 6 and 7) by an ill-conceived inclusion policy. Chapter 8 examines the government's response to evidence of workload pressure in the form of workforce reform which, as our evidence suggests, has impacted significantly on school structures but less so on hearts and minds. In the following chapter, we trace the roots of workload through successive government reforms and conclude that it is essentially in the hands of the profession itself to create reason in an unreasonable world.

 Questions for discussion

Teaching is not what it used to be. In what respects is that true? Have the lives of teachers changed for the better or for the worse?

To what extent is workload an explanatory factor for teachers, stress and dissatisfaction and to what extent are these explicable by other factors?

However bleak a picture we are offered of teaching in the twenty-first century, why do so many teachers still gain huge satisfaction from their job?

2

Balancing the Workload Equation: A Continuing Story

In this chapter, we adopt a historical perspective to examine how several decades of school reform, undertaken by governments of different persuasions, have resulted in the loss of teachers' autonomy in matters of *what* and *how* to teach, with the result that many teachers have come to believe that those in authority no longer trust their professional judgements in matters affecting their pupils' learning.

Among the public at large, teaching is often seen as an easy option. Some primary teachers we interviewed (Galton and MacBeath, 2002) said that they never owned up to being a teacher when asked at social gatherings what they did for a living. This was because admitting to being a teacher usually drew a response such as: 'Oh! Aren't you a lucky one with a nine to three job and all those lovely long holidays.'

At the same time there is a growing perception among the same public that teaching is not such a 'soft option' when it comes to dealing with unmotivated, badly behaved young adolescents, compounded by ever-increasing workload pressures. In England, this had led to a number of studies aimed at collecting precise information about the workloads of teachers. It was in the late sixties, however, that the workload question was opened by for wider debate, motivated by a desire to establish a competitive salary framework in relation to other professions. Accordingly, Harold Wilson's Labour Government commissioned the National Foundation of Educational Research (NFER) to carry out research, its findings contained in a report entitled, *The Teacher's Day* (Hilsum and Cane, 1971). Rather than using survey methods these researchers used direct observation and asked teachers in primary schools to keep diaries, recording evening, weekend and vacation activities. The study is important historically because the categories devised by Hilsum and Cane to break down the daily work of teachers have been used by subsequent researchers in both primary and secondary sectors in order to compare workloads of present and past generations of teachers. It also modelled the diarying approach now used in successive Teachers Workload Surveys, in which data is collected from primary and secondary school staff on a given week in March. This provides a complex picture of trends over the last six years and helps us track the impact of workload reform on the working lives of primary and secondary teachers, showing trends in number of hours worked and time given to various tasks in and out of school. (School Teachers' Review Body, 2000, 2003, 2004, 2005, 2006).

Opening the 'secret garden'

Prior to the election of the Thatcher Government in 1979, teachers had enjoyed a wide degree of autonomy in matters of curriculum and pedagogy, seen as 'a secret garden', particularly at the primary stage where the abandonment of the old 11-plus in the late sixties had led to a range of approaches as teachers sought pragmatic solutions to the problem of mixed ability classes. Although never as diverse and radical in practice as suggested by its critics, there were nevertheless 'pockets of progressive innovation' in areas such as Leicestershire, the West Riding and Oxfordshire (Alexander, 1995:286). Partly because concepts involved were often misunderstood and because research into classroom practice suggested that the rhetoric often outstripped the reality (Bennett, 1976; Galton *et al.*, 1980) James Callaghan's Labour Government called for a Great Debate, to open up the secret curriculum garden.

What followed, however, was more of a diatribe rather than a civilised discussion, with critics keen to assert, in the face of conflicting research evidence, that under the 'progressive revolution of the' sixties and seventies 'primary children were rarely taught anything but left to find out things for themselves'. This was essentially a broadside aimed at progressive primary schools but secondary schools did not escape the barrage of criticism, particular where secondary schools were beginning to reflect more of a primary ethos with open-plan design, cross-curricular work, project work, team teaching and even attempts at an integrated day (MacBeath, 1976).

By the time of Mrs Thatcher's third triumph at the polls the 'value for money' utilitarian and cost-cutting approach meant that the wheel had turned full circle.

In the primary sector curriculum values had become fully reminiscent of the 'elementary curriculum' of the late nineteenth century, writes Alexander (1995:16) while in the secondary sector critics such as Stephen Ball (2008:46) questioned how the goal of economic competitiveness was served by pedagogic strategies which were actually antithetical to the needs of a 'high skills' knowledge economy.

Although teachers may initially have been lulled into a 'false sense of security' by the National Curriculum Council's promise that these reforms merely represented 'what most practitioners were already doing', by the early 1990s protests had become more increasingly numerous with threats to boycott the National Testing programmes.

A primary cause for concern

A number of studies in the primary sector (Campbell and Neill, 1994; Galton and Fogelman, 1998; Woods *et al.*, 1997) all pointed to increasing dissatisfaction among teachers, in particular at changes which had taken place in the curriculum and in its assessment over the last decade. Campbell and Neill's (1994) research took place in the wake of the 1987 *Teachers' Pay and Conditions Act* which introduced the concept of directed time, requiring teachers to work not more than 195 days per year and to teach pupils for all but five days of this time. Directed time worked out at around 33 hours per week giving a total of 1,265 hours during an assumed 39-week working year. While teachers were portrayed as generally in favour of the new National Curriculum they were struggling to implement it, so that by 1993 the *dream* had become an emerging *nightmare* (Campbell and Neill, 1994:181). Campbell and Neill estimated that the time required for the core and foundation subjects exceeded the time available by just over two hours per week. They argued that those designing the curriculum had failed to take into account what termed *evaporated time*, that is, time notionally available for teaching but taken up by transitions from one location to another, such as supervising changing for PE or tidying up the classroom at the end of the day. Their estimate of this evaporated time came to 1.75 hours per week.

This study was one of the factors leading to Dearing's 1993 review of the National Curriculum and the introduction of '*discretionary*' and '*non-discretionary*' teaching time. Sir Ron Dearing's key recommendation was that 'the orders should be slimmed down' in order 'to free some 20 per cent of the teaching time for use at the discretion of the school' (paragraph 4.29). However, as Galton and Fogelman (1998:121) found, the idea of discretionary time was, in one head teacher's words 'a phantom 20 per cent really', since Ofsted inspectors tended to view the primary curriculum as an extension of the secondary model and looked unfavourably at any attempt to integrate aspects of literacy and numeracy into wider topic work. They preferred to be presented with a planned scheme of work with core and foundation subjects allocated distinct time slots. Added to this was the pressure to score well in the 'league tables' of National Curriculum Key Stage tests with the effect that most of the discretionary time was devoted to additional English and mathematics (p. 135) typically, between five and six hours per week against the notional time available of 4.7 hours. Teachers reported that they 'felt pressurised all the time' and were particularly anxious about slower learners who, because of the pressure to get through the curriculum, were 'rushed all the time', finding it 'extremely difficult to finish off pieces of work' (Galton and Fogelman, 1998:134).

In a detailed ethnographic study, Woods *et al.* (1997) noted that while teachers welcomed team work when planning the curriculum, 'enforced collaboration' and escalation in the number of meetings, resulted in 'killing off' much of the genuine collaboration that previously existed (Woods *et al.*, 1997:27). Most teachers interviewed had become compliant, accommodating imposed changes, surviving rather than developing professionally. The researchers pointed to statistics on increasing early retirement on the grounds of ill health as evidence of teachers' lack of professional satisfaction. Teachers under stress were most likely to be those with strong feelings of vocation, experiencing increasing role conflict between their personal and professional lives and above all with a sense that the personal values that they bought to their teaching were being undermined by the new orthodoxy (Woods *et al.*, 1997:146–154).

As these studies showed, the failure to account sufficiently for those aspects of the teacher's job which encroached into valued teaching time was the primary source of pressure. For teachers many of the tasks previously carried out at the end of the school day now had to be done in evenings or at weekends (Campbell and Neill, 1994:161).

Increasing the pressure: Education, education and more education

Many in the profession saw the new Labour Government as bringing a fresh approach and a welcome antidote to the events of the previous decade. However, the 1997 general election manifesto 'mantra' of education, education, education got off to an unpromising start when the new Secretary of State for Education began by naming and shaming 'the 18 worst schools' in the country. As reported by Liz Lightfoot, then education correspondent of the Daily Telegraph,

> Special consultants with proven records of turning schools round are to be sent in. Their £400-a-day fees will be paid by the Government. David Blunkett, the Education Secretary, gave warning that those who failed to raise standards would be closed and re-opened under a new name and possibly a new headteacher and change of staff. (21 May 1997)

Mr Blunkett's start was not auspicious. Although committed to a review of the National Curriculum (following the ending of the Dearing five-year moratorium) and reminding primary teachers, in particular, of the need for a 'balanced and broadly based curriculum' promoting the 'spiritual, moral, cultural, mental and physical development of pupils', he nevertheless announced a number of measures designed to ensure a focus on 'the basics' in order to meet the government's literacy and numeracy targets. Despite numerous warnings that the previous decade had produced a profession suffering from 'reform fatigue' (Campbell, 1998:96), in their first year of office the incoming government produced seven major bills and policy statements (Tomlinson, 2005). These included the setting up of the Standard and Effectiveness Unit, the launch of the 'New Deal' with the Summer Literacy Schools Initiative, the White Paper, *Excellence in Schools*, in which the National Literacy Strategy was announced (including a decision to devote one hour a day to literacy in all primary schools), the Schools Standards and Frameworks Bill, followed in the second year of government office in 1998 by Educational Action Zones, the National Grid for Learning, the Numeracy Taskforce, the publication of homework guidelines, the launching of Sure Start programmes for the zero to three-year-olds in areas of deprivation and the creation of Specialist and Beacon schools (later to become Leading Edge schools) and Excellence in Cities. This raft of government initiatives, new acts, new bodies (mostly consisting of nominated quangos or task forces), new green and white papers, thereafter continued apace.

Evaluating the impact of these policies on primary schools, Brehony (2005) notes that the thinking behind the Literacy and Numeracy Strategies appears to have had its origin in the 'third way' developed by Bill Clinton and the Democratic Party in the US. While previous Conservative governments had attempted to mandate prescribed teaching methods, in promoting their new strategies the Labour Government took matters considerably further.

One of the final acts of the Conservative government had been to set up the National Literacy Project in 1996, incorporating a dedicated literacy hour per day and an abandonment of individualised approaches in favour of whole class teaching. The emphasis on the 'back to basics' advocated by then Chief Inspector, Chris Woodhead (whose continuing tenure did nothing to reassure the profession) meant that there was an increase in the mechanics of reading and writing with greater emphasis on both phonics and grammar. Just as the Literacy Taskforce emphasised grammar and the mechanics of writing, so the Numeracy group gave a similar priority to calculation skills. In both cases, the focus was on whole class teaching largely based on the various reviews by Ofsted (for example, Reynolds and Farrell, 1996), despite challenges to the claim that the Literacy and Numeracy Strategies represented the best 'evidence-based practice' (Brown *et al.*, 1998; Alexander, 2004). In the following years, mounting concern was expressed about the rigidity of the strategies, primary teachers struggling to fit the rest of the curriculum into the timetable, given that ten hours of the 25 hours of primary schooling per week were now taken up by mathematics and English.

According to Brehony (2005:39) anxieties were expressed elsewhere in government, 'that an overly dirigiste approach to the management of teachers and an overly explicit classroom pedagogy would do little to release the creativity and innovation which the knowledge-based economy would require.' Others such as Bentley (1998) then a director of the think-tank, DEMOS (heavily influential in Labour's thinking) expressed similar concerns, arguing that the emphasis on paper qualifications should be reduced and that the skills needed for 'the new knowledge economy' should be integrated into mainstream teaching.

A secondary story and the standards myth

There is little obvious relationship between skills needed for the knowledge economy and the reduction in secondary school curriculum subjects which followed The Dearing Committee's 1994 recommendation. It was arts and humanities that were sacrificed in order to create for a vocational pathway and a renewed emphasis on the 'core' subjects. This was the legacy of the incoming Labour government, by that time so firmly embedded that the Conservative reforms remained essentially intact. David Blunkett instructed the Qualifications and Curriculum Authority to 'avoid excessive disruption and upheaval in the curriculum' so as to focus exclusively on what needed to be done to raise standards (Davies and Edwards, 2001). As these authors point out:

> Under New Labour 'standards' have replaced 'curriculum' as the discursive hub of educational policy making. And this discursive reorientation has legitimated the obsessive setting and pursuit of pre-specified targets... Moreover, it simplistically assumes that the targets can be met by what is taken to be 'proven best practice' (p. 99).

As in the primary sector more and more time was needed after school to compensate for subjects that had become squeezed out of the timetable, with study support, homework clubs, breakfast clubs, weekend schools and summer schools providing opportunities for revisiting of core subjects with after hours support by teachers and other staff (MacBeath *et al.*, 2001). While many study centres provided alternative approaches, encouraging self-directed and collaborative learning, this ran counter to the wishes of HMCI Woodhead who argued for more directive additional teaching.

The counsel against an excessively dirigiste approach to the management of teachers and an overly explicit classroom pedagogy appears to have cut little ice as the government declared itself unwilling 'to defend the failings of across-the-board mixed ability teaching' (DfEE, 1997:37), announcing that setting should be the norm in secondary schools. This, despite any lack of evidence that setting is more likely to 'raise standards' or 'close the gap' than mixed ability teaching. Terry Wrigley (2003:97) charges policy makers with being; 'in denial' as 'paradoxically, in England, it is now the very schools which are succeeding least with the National Curriculum that have the least scope for departing from it.'

The inflexibility of curriculum and testing work systemically against worthwhile learning for those young people who need it most. A study of eight secondary schools 'in exceptionally challenging circumstances' (MacBeath *et al.*, 2006) found that despite huge government investment, resourcing, training and intervention, evidence of improvement was equivocal among these eight schools with one of them (the Ridings) eventually closing and another being returned to special measures. As the study concluded:

> Our ultimate concern lies with the conception of an intervention that was too narrowly and inwardly focused, too impatient to get to grips with nature of the challenging circumstances themselves. One of the burdens the schools who signed up for it had to endure was that they ran the risk of becoming victims of expectations that were, on the one hand, overly ambitious, and on the other, too short sighted.

> Seeking to prescribe the 'what and how' of school improvement in widely differing institutions and social contexts can be counter productive. Change starts to take root in schools when the staff collectively began to get hold of a 'powerful idea'. That idea could take a variety of different forms. Policy-makers need to become more adept at drawing up menus of the most promising ideas which schools may approach as 'a la carte', while ordering 'off-menu' should be also examined and appraised on its merits (p. 155).

Addressing the workload issue

As implementation of new initiatives continued unabated the issue of 'workloads' had became an increasingly preoccupying concern by the turn of the century. In acknowledgement of decreasing morale and a retention, recruitment 'crisis', the government commissioned their own study into teachers' working conditions.

In 2001 the accountants, PricewaterhouseCooper (PwC, 2001) were asked to identify the main factors determining teachers' and head teachers' workload, and to develop a programme of practical action to eliminate excessive workload. This was set within an overall aim 'to promote the most effective use of all resources in schools in order to raise standards of pupil achievement'.

The study involved fieldwork in 102 schools, discussions with national and local bodies, and a benchmarking of teachers' hours against other UK occupations and against overseas teachers. Out of this emerged a number of substantive issues for the Government and the profession to address, also setting in train the continuing biannual review of workload by the school teachers' review body.

The key finding of the PwC study was that teachers and head teachers worked more intensive weeks than other comparable managers and professionals.

Teachers without management responsibilities worked around 52 hours each week during term time, compared with around 45 hours for managers and professionals in other occupations across the UK, a weekly workload that teachers taking part in the PricewaterhouseCooper survey also regarded as a reasonable commitment. When hours were compared on an annual basis levels of work were fairly similar to other comparable professions but it was the intensity of the working week, however, that emerged as the significant issue. The following findings are significant as they were highly influential in identifying the range of pressures on teachers and setting out the stall for the workforce remodelling that was to follow.

Teaching was described as an unique and unusual profession and teachers who were interviewed underlined some of its peculiar features:

- At the core of the job was the need to put on a 'performance' for many hours each day. This while it could at times be exhilarating was also often exhausting.
- There was relatively little contact with other adults so that some teachers may have virtually no time for a conversation with another adult during a whole day.
- The working environment was often a source of pressure in itself with lack of suitable space, often inadequate resources and support.
- Lack of availability of Information and Communications Technology (ICT) resources, lack of support and suitable training lent to skill gaps and increased workload.
- Lack of opportunity to share experiences, expertise and software among schools was often compounded by a lack of compatibility between different data management software packages and accessibility to existing web-based resources.
- Not being in control of their work was a salient cause of stress, exacerbated by the pace and manner of change, insufficient support to meet those changes and resentment about having to engage in tasks which did not support learning. Tasks carried into weekends were an additional source of resentment.
- Many tasks could be carried out by staff rather than by teachers, or more efficiently using ICT. As professionals, teachers felt they had not been accorded the trust they merited. Finding the right balance between accountability and trust would therefore entail reduced requirements for documentation, greater capacity for local innovation and risk-taking.
- Inappropriate expectation of what schools and teachers could achieve intensified pressure, especially in a context of deteriorating pupil behaviour and a lack of parental support. Head teachers did not always recognise the need to manage the workload of their staff and the drive for higher standards was not always balanced by attention to sustainable workloads.
- Head teachers' own workloads were higher than average by some 300–400 hours a year in comparison to other professions (even after taking account of holiday hours). They too experienced intense pressure of high expectations

and levels of accountability (in particular through Ofsted inspection reports and performance tables).

- The timing and quality of Continuing Professional Development (CPD) added to workload and lifestyle problems. Training during the school day required supply cover, with attendant concerns about support for classes, plus the additional extra preparation and marking that this generated. Training in twilight sessions, on the other hand, meant that teachers were tired after a working day as well as the additional weekly hours this approach generated.

The PricewaterhouseCooper (PwC, 2001:32) report concluded as follows:

> On the basis of the issues above and our many discussions with school staff in the course of this work we believe there are serious risks attached to not addressing these issues, some of which need to be addressed in the near future. These include that the considerable investment being made in schools will not have the desired impact due to poor teacher morale, lower retention rates and that school managers will not be able to continue to respond to demands for change. This ultimately could impact on pupil attainment.

Constructing a future agenda

There are many valuable insights into the issues surrounding teachers' workload emanating from the PwC survey but the proposed solutions were largely managerial and technical paid little attention to the impact on existing school and teaching cultures. Recommending greater use of unqualified personnel to carry out more mundane classroom tasks overlooked the longstanding contentious debate among teachers about the nature and status of the profession, and in particular the tasks which classroom assistants should be permitted to perform.

The four studies commissioned by the National Union of Teachers between 2002 and 2007 explored these issues, casting our net wider than the working conditions of teachers and setting the emerging issues within an international context. Across the globe research indicates that the lives of teachers are more stressful and that there is a growing imbalance between their work and personal lives. In the UK, teachers see pressures as emanating from centralised reforms accompanied by excessive bureaucratic procedures. In Australia and Canada, however, where central government has little control over education policy teachers also complain of similar pressures. In Hong Kong where government reform has been to reduce central control and give more freedom to schools workloads are in excess of those reported elsewhere. It would seem likely therefore that there is a variety of explanations to account for workload pressures. In the final analysis, any serious attempt to provide a more attractive working life for teachers needs to start from what is in their power to change and what is critical for them to retain. Rather than waiting for educational systems to change – for the educational world to become a reasonable one – the pre-eminent task is to work out what can be improved in an unreasonable world.

 Questions for discussion

Where should the balance lie between central government and schools in matters concerning curriculum and teaching?

How far have the suggested revisions of the primary and secondary strategies helped to ameliorate the workloads of teachers and school leaders?

Has the period since the implementation of the PricewaterhouseCooper report resulted in a better work-life balance for teachers?

3

A Life in Teaching: The Primary Teacher's Experience?

In this chapter, we look at work-life balance of English primary teachers through the accounts of three practitioners representing different backgrounds and range of experience. In every case, although long hours are a feature of their dissatisfaction with their job, it is the underlying frustration to do with 'intensification' and the feeling of not 'being trusted as professionals' that give rise to growing disillusion with a life in teaching.

What has changed?

What has been the impact of changes in the National Curriculum, key stage assessment and the introduction of literacy and numeracy strategies in the life and work of teachers? A raft of studies have all pointed to increasing dissatisfaction among primary teachers but as earlier studies have also shown, teachers have always stayed on after school and worked at home in the evenings and weekends. So what has changed? Three decades ago a considerable amount of after-school activity was devoted to putting up displays or preparing materials for future lessons, a longstanding, collaborative activity in primary schools (Hilsum and Cane, 1971:187). It had the merit of bringing together teachers from a particular year group to talk about the quality of pupils' work while mounting a joint display. It was a time for conversations about pupils or exchange of advice about different teaching approaches. However, the PricewaterhouseCoopers study recommended that such tasks should be transferred to administrative staff (PwC, 2001:50). While from an outsider's perspective it may appear reasonable to identify tasks which, because of their apparently mechanical nature, could be delegated to less qualified personnel, this is to misunderstand the nature of teachers' work. It cannot be simply disaggregated into administrative and pedagogic tasks. However, these kinds of 'collegial' exchanges, highly valued by primary teachers, appear now to be all too rare. Attempts to ameliorate some of the problems identified in the working lives of teachers need to start from a recognition that what at first sight appears mundane and routine can often have important cultural, intellectual and social consequences.

Three teachers' stories

Workload data tells only a partial story. They provide a broad sweep of issues but provide little insight into what it means for the individual teacher. They can only hint at what it means to balance the demands of home, work, family and friends. In this chapter, therefore, we try to give a flavour of the human impact through stories told by teachers we met in the course of our original primary survey. The three teachers we have called Penny, Mark and Miriam. We do not claim they are a representative sample but we have chosen them to suggest a range of teaching experience, different settings and at different points on their career path. We are confident, however, that these stories reflect the pressures affecting their colleagues in primary schools across the country.

Penny, the career enthusiast

Penny has been a teacher for 20 years. She teaches a Year 3/4 class in a rural primary school with 150 children. She is also Deputy Head, Science, DT and Inset Co-ordinator. She is in her forties.

Hours of work
Penny arrives at school at least an hour before the children and leaves two to three hours after the school day. With her lunchtime being used almost entirely for work, she estimates that on top of teaching time she is working in school for 47 hours weekly. Having arrived home in the evening she will eat and have a couple of hours off before sitting down for another two to three hours work. At weekends she tries to have Friday and Saturday off and then on Sunday will often work for another five hours. In total this makes for a 60-hour working week.

No non-contact time
Despite all her added responsibilities, non-contact does not exist. Non-teaching time is spent on meetings, organising resources and marking, and paperwork

associated with these roles is carried out in the evenings and at weekends. Penny feels frustrated that she is unable to fulfil all her responsibilities as Subject Co-ordinator as there is no time to monitor children's learning in other classes. She also regrets that there is no time for herself and her colleagues to observe one another and share practice. Non-contact time would be one of the main initiatives that would help Penny manage her workload.

> I would use it for monitoring, that would be my main area. The opportunity to get into other classes to monitor children's work and obviously evaluating my own work because that takes up a lot of time too after your lessons.

Non-contact time is not helpful, however, if the class teacher then has to spend precious time preparing for a supply teacher. The huge amount of work expected of teachers if they leave their class means that many choose not to attend outside courses.

> When you're off on a course, gone are the days when you could leave the supply teachers and say well you bring in your own material and decide what you want to do. Everything has to be planned for that supply because you know that if you leave it for a day, you're another day behind and you've got to catch up somewhere along the line.

Increase in paperwork

The biggest change in Penny's workload over the last 20 years is the amount of paperwork. Apart from taking up time it also reduces her energy levels and she finds her teaching suffering. She does not mind paperwork that has a clear purpose and educational benefit, but much of it is unnecessary and she resents its time-consuming nature.

> I don't mind if the paperwork is purposeful. The problems arise when I feel I'm literally filling in a form for the sake of filling in a form. It is not going anywhere, it is not informing anybody and that is when the resentment comes in. I feel is this just sitting in someone's filing cabinet somewhere?

Loss of confidence

The pace of externally imposed systems in the form of new initiatives has seriously undermined Penny's confidence. While appreciative of many of the new initiatives she is unhappy at the lack of respect given to her expertise and professional knowledge.

> I felt my confidence suddenly going. I felt deskilled as if everything we had been doing all these years, in a way it was almost like the government saying, 'You haven't been doing it well enough. This is how it should be done now. This is what we're prescribing. This is what we want you to deliver.' That was a hindrance because my confidence was suddenly plummeting again and that had to be built up.

Loss of time to develop children's interest/Loss of time to listen

Penny's working conditions leave little flexibility within the teaching day. There is less and less possibility for extending periods of learning or answering children's questions because of the pressures to teach a full curriculum. Many aspects of learning now feel rushed, with less scope for spontaneity and less time to talk to and listen to children, for her, a crucial aspect of a primary school education as well as the most enjoyable part of teaching.

> It's the spontaneity that's gone. I mean if it had snowed we used to run to the window and we'd stop and do some creative poetry. That's gone now because everything is very much structured now, very planned and that's a shame.

> Another thing is you're losing the one-to-one contact time through this time constraint. Gone are the days when you could sit down and really get to know the children and talk to them on a one-to-one basis. It's either very much group-based or whole class.

Loss of social life

Penny manages this heavy load by having a curtailed social life. It helps that she has no children of her own. In the past she was able to teach and maybe enjoy other pursuits twice a week. However, it now eats into her leisure time. If she did socialise more she fears her work would suffer. She would get behind and her stress levels would rise.

> I have a very reduced social life. Before, I could very much explore my own interests. In previous years I have attended night classes but I had to drop those, I swam once a week but I find that slipping out now.

Mark, the teacher who's getting out

Mark has been teaching for 11 years. He currently works in an inner city school with 400 children. He is a Year 6 teacher and Music Co-ordinator. In the past he had a management role within the school but decided to drop that due to the 'unbearable pressure' it caused. Mark is in his early thirties, and was interviewed as part of a group and therefore had less speaking time. Mark's story is an amalgamation of a few teachers in their early thirties who, like him, were planning to leave teaching or go part-time.

Leaving teaching

Mark is leaving teaching at the end of the year. He reflects that teaching is now a profession where there is 'nowhere else for him to go'. He is exhausted and wants to pursue other aspects of his life that he feels have been neglected over the last few years. Like Penny, the long hours he spends in the evenings and weekends on schoolwork means there are fewer opportunities to develop his interests.

> It's a lifestyle change. I'm looking for a career with more levels of satisfaction and I want to be challenged by things that I want to be challenged by. At the moment I just feel challenged by everything. I want to be challenged by things which I feel have real value.

> The planning and preparation is immense! I am very fed up. Friends who graduated at the same time as myself are valued and get weekends off because they are not teachers! I must get a life!

Health problems
Mark is tired. The constant feeling of exhaustion prevents him leading a full life. He also feels undervalued and demoralised by the lack of encouragement, praise and support.

> There is copious and needless paperwork which on top of your preparation and marking and getting resources organised leaves you demoralised and physically and mentally drained.

Pressure of SATs
Being a Year 6 teacher, Mark experiences a great deal of pressure to achieve 'acceptable' results in the SATs. For the whole spring term and early summer term his main focus has been in getting children through the SATs, which he finds stressful and unrewarding. It also means subjects other than Literacy, Numeracy and Science get squeezed, making the curriculum very limited.

> I feel I've got a lot of pressure on me to keep the level of improvement that's been going on going. It's really hard to squeeze a year 6 programme in given that it really does feel as though it's all about levels and targets.

> I think if you're not careful everything is geared to one week in May and I question the value of it. Is that what education is about? I don't think it is. I think you don't end up delivering a broad and balanced curriculum because I think your whole focus is on Science, Maths and English because that's what you're being tested on and we put a lot of pressure on the children and on ourselves.

Curriculum: Loss of creativity and spontaneity
The pressures to meet targets has deeply affected Mark's job satisfaction. There is now no time for the sustained and creative activities he and his pupils once enjoyed.

> I think it's too prescriptive and the timetabling of it is too limiting and it's taken away a lot of stuff that I think we used to do very well like book making and extended writing. And reading when do the kids really really read now?

> The creative stuff is going isn't it; the art, the building, designing, making. Also we used to do a lot more learning that started with children bringing something in so it didn't matter what you had planned for the day. All of a sudden your day was focussed around this thing, it was spontaneous and fun.

Mark also worries that the highly structured day puts a lot of pressure on children. He thinks that the rise in the number of disruptive children, that sap his energy, is partly due to the overemphasis on content and an inflexible day.

> Backchat and tantrums now seem to be a daily feature of classroom life. Is it just because kids are worse or is it their reaction to a curriculum that has become more pressured, more driven with less room to be off-task?

Resources

The school does not always have the resources that Mark needs to make his lessons fun and creative as most of the resources are swallowed up by the literacy and numeracy strategies. So he finds himself going out and buying card, glue, stickers and also trailing around to procure freebies. 'This constant need to dig into my own pocket, to scrabble around for resources really, really gets to me'.

Classroom resources often come too late so that there is very little time to review what is on offer. He is therefore dependent on handouts.

> What I find really annoying in Year 6 is that you get a lot of these brochures and handouts and flyers about how to teach this, or preparing for the planning of SATs, and they always come about two months after you've started teaching it. It's like no-one thinks in time, and I find that really frustrating.

Miriam, the demoralised teacher

Miriam has been teaching for 20 years. She currently works as a Reception teacher for 0.8 of her time in an inner city school. Miriam is in her forties.

Hours of work

Typically, Miriam arrives at school by 8 a.m. and leaves around 6 p.m. Evening work and weekend work is the norm. The time before school is used for preparing resources and setting out the classroom. She also uses some of this time to brief classroom assistants about tasks for the day. At lunchtime she tries to sit down for ten minutes but is usually either getting things ready for the afternoon session or doing administrative tasks. At the end of the day there are meetings twice a week and planning and assessment tasks. Miriam tries to do as much work as she can before going home although she often finds herself doing work in the evening in front of the telly. Sunday afternoon are used to do all the planning for the following week. If she doesn't do this then her evenings in that week become much fuller.

> I would like to be able to leave the building sometimes and think I don't have to think about this job until I come back into it again and I find I can never do that. I resent that. If a weekend goes by and I haven't done school work it's like, 'God, when am I going to find the time to do it now?' So that's why it's midnight Tuesday, midnight Wednesday to gather up the time that I could have done on Sunday afternoon.

> It's my own social life, I find, has diminished; especially when you've got your own family as well. You think, well, my family needs to come first really and, and then you're stuck behind sorting out assessments and things. I think in the past, report writing took up a lot of your time, outside time, and I was prepared to give up three weeks of my time solid, but now you've got other things coming in like assessment and you're giving up more of your time, you know. And I think out of everything you don't have a life, really. Even the holidays, you're thinking about what you're doing for the next term. I would say the only real break I actually get, to stop thinking about teaching, is in that six weeks block. But then you've got your last week towards the end of the six weeks holiday. I'm always in during that last week as well.

Increase in stress

Miriam finds it increasingly hard to find time to 'switch off' from her heavy workload. Balancing the intensity of work with time to relax and recharge seems a constantly elusive goal. She is unable ever to feel as though she is 'on top of it all'.

> It's hard to switch off and when you're not doing it [school work] you're very aware that you must find some time to do this but when you're trying to have a life it's like it's always there.

> We're not quite good enough. You never get to the end of your list of things you're supposed to be doing. You put all these hours in and you've still not finished it. And you never ever get to finish it and I find that an ongoing battle really.

The increasing amount of work Miriam is doing at home has at times put pressure on her family life and her relationship with her partner.

> He can get quite cross at times to be perfectly honest. He'll say, 'Do you *really* have to do this?' But I think he's concerned about me to be honest. He can see I'm extremely tired a lot of time.

Loss of control

The diminishing feeling of being control in a profession she once loved has fuelled Miriam's sense of despondency. Her opinions and expertise aren't respected and she feels overloaded by things that external agencies have told her to do, and resentful of the increasing amount of time it takes.

> I just don't feel like you're trusted anymore. I think at one time you were very autonomous and that was the great thing about teaching. That is a buzz and a

plus about it. It's you and those kids. Now it's just pressure isn't it to fill in the boxes or whatever and I think that affects the performance you can give with the children.

The new initiatives, even though tackling some important issues, have led increasingly to set ways of planning and delivering lessons and Miriam worries that this not only limits children's educational experience but diminishes teachers' creativity and spontaneity. She believes that this is a reason for many good teachers leaving the profession.

> That's what we always remember about teachers that taught us. It's the personalities of them and the love of what they were doing that they brought to it and if you start to squash that out of people what sort of teachers are you going to create? And they are the teachers who have gone, who have gone, and sometimes when you stay you think 'Oh God there's something wrong with me I'm still here! Why am I still here?' I know people who have just said I can't do it. I'm not doing it and they're not going to.

For newly qualified teachers (NQTS) the emphasis on structured lesson plans, the over-reliance on a set way of delivery, left no room for creativity or alternative ways of doing things.

> I think there's a danger of taking away teachers creativity as well and I see newly qualified teachers coming through now and they have no experience of that. Brilliant at delivering the literacy hours and very slick and great you know, something I'll never be able to do and I've got something to learn from them about that, but they've not been exposed to other ways of doing things and there is more than one way, more than one path to get to the end product.

Support

Miriam works with no full-time learning support assistant (LSA) but has three who are in and out of the classroom through the week, some who work specifically with one child. Although she benefits from adult contact and support in the classroom, the management of all the extra adults adds to workload.

> It's an inclusive school, we have a whole range of children with disabilities and they come with a lot of extra adults. In one way that makes more work for us as teachers because we have to liaise with all these people that we're working with and manage them as well. But I think that having lots of adults around you as a worker means that you're not working with children on your own all the time and that's a good thing.

Three teachers – common cause, common causes

Three teachers, at different stages in their career, different in their personalities and family contexts, holding different levels of responsibility within their schools. All are unknown to one another but share a common cause and common cause for concern.

In their choice of words they reveal much of themselves and the changing nature of their work. The word 'time' occurs eight times in these accounts. Tired, exhausted, 'drained' or 'lack or energy' occur six times. There are six references to pressure and three to stress. The desire for a social life, or just 'a life' receives five mentions. Other words with emotional force are 'demoralised', 'struggling', 'resentment', confidence as 'plummeting' and references to teaching as a 'battle'.

This vocabulary of embattlement is juxtaposed with references to spontaneity, fun, creativity, all as aspects of teaching that are seen to be lost. Miriam describes the love of teaching being 'squashed' out of people. She no longer feels trusted to do her job effectively. Penny, an experienced teacher talks about being deskilled, by a government saying to her 'You haven't been doing it well enough. This is how it should be done now.' Mark, who will be lost to teaching, might have felt differently if even the 'little things' had been done to reward his commitment and effort, small tokens that teachers are valued.

In the personal accounts we can therefore detect the same recurring themes identified in the earlier studies presented in Chapter 2. However, the interviews with these primary teachers took place shortly before the National Agreement for remodelling of the workforce came into force (DfES, 2003b).

In 2007, we revisited these schools and spoke to some of the teachers who had taken part in our earlier interviews. We wanted to discover how far the reforms, particularly the decision to provide statutory planning and preparation time in all primary school, had made life more bearable for staff and removed some of the cause of resentment and stress as perceived by Miriam, Mark and Penny. The next chapter describes what we found.

 ## Questions for discussion

How far do you feel that the sentiments expressed by these three teachers are representative of the primary profession in general?

Irrespective of government policy, what can schools, themselves, do to encourage teachers like Mark, in mid-career, to stay on in teaching?

Do you think that teachers who refuse to delegate putting up classroom displays to an assistant have only themselves to blame for excessive workloads?

4

Remodelling the Primary Teaching Workforce

What changes that have taken place in the primary schools we visited five years earlier, shortly before the introduction of the National Workforce Agreement? The biggest change to the teachers' working lives has come from the introduction of planning, preparation and assessment (PPA) time. While broadly welcomed there was ambivalence about the role of teaching assistants (TAs) in covering teachers' time out of the classroom. Nor did additional non-contact time necessarily appear to reduce teachers' overall weekly workload, nor the amount of time spent during evenings and weekends. Why this should be so is discussed in the chapter.

What has changed in primary teaching?

We first surveyed primary schools in 2002, the year before the workload agreement came into operation. Five years later on our return visits to the same schools we wanted to discover how things might have changed. To what extent was remodelling:

- Relieving teachers of administrative tasks?
- Offering support through appointment of non-teaching staff?
- Lessening the workload?
- Creating more opportunities for professional development?
- Bringing about a better work-life balance?

Whenever possible we interviewed the same teachers. Of the five schools visited two were in inner city areas (one south and one north), one was rural and two were located in suburban areas. Of these latter two schools, one was situated on the edge of large industrial city in the East Midlands and the other was near a market town in a large agricultural county. We typically interviewed the head teacher, the SENCO, six class teachers, some with management responsibilities and four or five teaching assistants. In all, therefore, we talked with around 60 individuals.

We began our interviews with teachers by asking them to describe a typical day, assessing how much time was spent on school work during the evenings and at weekends. Most teachers pointed out that this latter time varied enormously according to the period in the year. The bulk of medium-term planning, particularly for literacy, tended to be done during the holidays so there was less to do at the beginning of term. Report writing towards the end of term could take up four hours in an evening and ten hours at weekends. Given that most of the teachers were in school by 8.30 a.m. and didn't leave until around 5.30 p.m., and that they usually didn't work Friday evenings, this adds up to a 75-hour week at certain times of the year. For teachers with responsibilities such as drawing up policy documents or bidding for Health School Awards or Creative Partnerships this often required additional out-of-school time.

Typically teachers came in between 7.45 a.m. and 8.15 a.m. and spent the time before classes setting up for the day. A quick ten-minute break mid-morning, 20 minutes for lunch, before leaving home between 5 p.m. and 6 p.m. meant that the typical working day lasted around nine hours (excluding lunch and morning breaks). When not teaching, apart from the allocated PPA time, teachers took clubs, either at lunchtime or after school. On average these teachers were involved in three such activities.

Compared with the 2002 survey we found an increase in the typical hours worked from just over 54 hours a week to 56 hours. This figure is based on the assumption that school work which might have been done on a Friday evening is carried over to the weekend. Most evening work is preparation or marking. Weekends are mainly reserved for short-term planning for the following week, catching up with records and other administrative chores.

> Literacy planning takes a long time to do and also when you've got a class where there's so many...you know, where the range is great. It is planning for that differentiation, planning for the whole week. (Year 5 teacher)

> With the little ones you tend to do practical things, like buy some boxes, or buy some seeds, or you know, but they have to be done.... With the little ones you are sort of preparing visual things and laminating and all that takes a bit of time... I would say five or six hours. (Reception class teacher)

Interestingly, these latter tasks are the kinds of activities included in the 24 administrative tasks that teachers are supposed to have ceased to do under the remodelling agreement.

Table 4.1   Average hours worked by primary teachers (1971–2006).
OME (2006), Teacher's Workload Diary Survey, London: Office of Manpower &
Economics

Activity	Hilsum & Cane (1971) [hours]	Campbell & Neill (1994) [hours]	Galton & MacBeath (2002) [hours]	OME (2006) [hours]
Teaching	18.8	22	24.2	16.8
Preparation/planning/marking	4.3	17.2	14.2	12.6
Administration/other	11.5	7.3	6.6	4.8
Dealing with parents/pupils	6.0	2.8	3.2	5.5
After-school work	0.7	1.1	1.2	6.6
Weekend work	3.3	3.2	5.4	3.8
Total	44.6	53.6	54.8	50.1

Nearly all the teachers interviewed claimed that they were now working longer than when we visited five years earlier. This contradicts the Office of Manpower and Economics (OME, 2006) calculations shown in Table 4.1. In examining the table the emphasis should be on the trends rather than the individual categories used in the OME surveys. This is because how time is categorised differs from survey to survey. Thus in the Hilsum and Cane (1971) study there was no separate category for meeting with parents other than formal parents evenings, so other meetings are subsumed within informal activities, including conversations with colleagues and pupils.

Whereas the OME (2006) figure for after-school work is higher than Campbell and Neill (1994) and Galton and MacBeath (2002), the latter two studies only specified after-school clubs with other forms of non-contact time in school after 3.30 p.m. included in the preparation, planning and marking category. Thus in Table 4.1, the 'other' category has been used to include all activities which could not be placed elsewhere. This accounts for the apparently anomalous finding that in Hilsum and Cane's time teachers appeared overwhelmed by administrative tasks.

The figure for teaching in the OME survey, based on their finding that both primary and secondary teachers 'spend just over a third of their time on teaching activities', appears somewhat puzzling, even allowing for the impact of PPA time, as is the claim that secondary teachers do more teaching than primary colleagues.

A typical day's timetable might see 9.00 a.m. till 9.30 a.m. taken up by registration and assembly. Lessons would then proceed until 12.30 p.m. with a 15-minute mid-morning break. An hour's lunch break would mean school starting at 1.30 p.m. and finishing around 3.00 p.m. or 3.15 p.m. depending on whether there was another break in mid-afternoon. At a minimum, therefore, primary pupils are being taught for 21.25 hours per week and in many schools, where time for assemblies has been reduced to one per week, this could rise to 23 hours. Even allowing for a generous allocation of a whole afternoon PPA time (as was the case in most of the schools visited in the 2007 case studies) this leaves 18.75 hours to be accounted for. Either this missing time 2 hours (18.75–16.8) is a statistical artefact of merging full- and part-time teaching loads or is being covered by specialist teachers for subjects such as music and ICT or is allocated to a teaching assistant.

Two things stand out in the table. First, the time given to parents and dealing with pupils' problems has increased, particularly since in the earlier surveys most of this time was taken up in dealing with pupils' problems. In our 2002 survey, for example, only 0.9 out of the 3.2 hours per week was taken up with parents. If we then add planning time to after-school hours (since in the earlier surveys much of after-school work was subsumed within the planning category) then workloads have increased since 2002. For the OME (2006) survey the combined figure is 16.7 hours (12.6 + 6.6 – 2.5 hours PPA time). Our corresponding figure is 15.4 hours (1.2 + 14.2 hours). To find out why these increases have occurred we need to look at what teachers told us in our recent school visits.

You can't do dinosaurs and castles – oh yes you can!

One of the main changes which have taken place since our first survey has been the attempt to develop a skill-based approach to the primary curriculum as part of the new primary strategy following on from the publication of *Excellence and enjoyment: A strategy for primary schools* (DfES, 2003a). Ironically, this approach of attempting to embed aspects of literacy and numeracy teaching into other subjects was the strategy adopted by the Interim Primary Committee, which was set up in 1988 to prepare for the creation of the National Curriculum. However, this idea was rejected by the then Secretary of State for Education who favoured 'a subject approach' to curriculum building and insisted that primary schools should provide pupils with a real knowledge of history 'rather than being taught dinosaurs for the second or third time' (Baker, 1993:193). Moreover, he rejected the idea of a committee of primary specialists to oversee the construction of Key Stages 1 and 2 and instead put a primary representative on the various Subject Committees dominated by secondary specialist (Galton, 1995:28). The inevitable result was to produce an overcrowded timetable, made worse by the statutory requirement under the Labour Government, requiring primary schools to devote two out of the 4.5 hours of each day's teaching to literacy and numeracy. Teachers in the 2002 survey resented this straitjacket as the following quotations illustrate:

> The expectation of the amount that has to be covered, that needs to be really slimmed down. Doesn't it? It feels all the time you are rushing to deliver a huge curriculum that you've been told to deliver that doesn't end up balanced because of the pressure on literacy and numeracy, which come from the pressure for results so there're not getting sufficient time on the other subjects. [Deputy Head, 11 years' experience] (Galton and MacBeath, 2002:38)

> You feel obliged to fit into a timetabled structure and it isn't always possible with practical subjects, like Art and Design Technology. You can't do that and part of

> you feels guilty that you're not teaching how you used to teach. You feel quite stressed about it. [Teacher, 20 years' experience] (Galton and MacBeath, 2002:39)

The schools in our 2007 case study appeared to be emerging from under the dark cloud of this dutiful and mechanistic approach to the National Curriculum and QCA's (Qualifications and Curriculum Authority) prescriptions. In one of the schools visited, the head was endeavouring to challenge teachers who appeared too scared to depart from what they still saw, wrongly, as mandated subjects. He was attempting to liberate them to work from children's interests towards the NC rather than in the opposite direction. Long-serving staff, of which there were many, described a pendulum swing from the early thematic work they were used to, to adopt the straitjacket of the Key Stage Strategies and Literacy and Numeracy and now back again, or indeed forward, with more insight and structure to a interdisciplinary learner-centred approach. Teachers at this school ascribed the change both to visionary leadership and to some extent a general lightening of policy directive. Nonetheless the policy climate was still seen as too 'next step orientated', and the constant target orientation often meant that 'children switched off too quickly', particularly those with a short attention span who looked for continuous stimulation and reinforcement. Similar views were expressed in another of our schools:

> I think the pressures have changed. Now there is the assessment targets, class targets. You assess naturally but it's all the paperwork associated with it. It's so time consuming. That has really changed in the last two or three years. [Key Stage 1 teacher]

> I think some of the things that have come through… it's [marking] has got more not less. Although you would assess everybody… all teachers were assessing the whole time, it's now more into, well, it's got to be assessed on this type of thing, it's got to be assessed on that. There are registers, I mean like the Gifted and Talented. That's a great initiative but then we were having to put on children from every year group so it's not just the teacher getting the registers but we're collecting the registers and we have meetings with all these people to go through them. So there seems to be more and more. (Deputy Head and Year 6 teacher)

One Key Stage 2 teacher who was also Literacy co-ordinator summed up the prevailing sentiment.

> I would want to change the constant assessment. I really do feel I'm constantly assessing and at the end of the day you don't see the child as a person – you see them as a target which is really, really sad.

A further problem concerns less experienced teachers who have, themselves, been taught under the National Curriculum and have then been trained to teach it. One Deputy Head teacher cited the example of putting a dinosaur on a desk in front of a student teacher who didn't know what to do with it. She cited him as a symbol of the age of compliance, so that teacher mentors now have to induct students and NQTs into a more child-centred culture. This again requires time.

Parents under pressure

In all the schools that we visited head teachers and staff commented on the difficulties with a small but significant group of parents. These parents, themselves under social pressure and often unable to deal with their own children's behaviour could be highly confrontational, sometimes resorting to violence in protecting their children's interests. While these parents were a minority, verbal threats and promises of 'going up to the civic' could shake a teacher's confidence and have an emotional ripple effect through the rest of the day.

Teachers described 'highly permissive' parents who admitted to indulging their children, often for the sake of peace or simply because they had run out alternative incentives or sanctions. They described incidents such as

- The mother who with great effort has now succeeded in getting her five-year-old to bed at 1 a.m. instead of 3 a.m.
- The seven-year-old who threw his PlayStation against the wall in a tantrum then had tantrums for a week until his mother bought him a new one.
- A six-year-old who told his teacher how to go about killing pimps and prostitutes after mastering *The Grand Theft Auto* in which the player has to kill as many people as possible.
- Parents who can't say no to their children demanding televisions, computers in their bedrooms, taking meals on their own and being isolated from the rest of the family.
- Parents who will do anything to shut their children up 'just to get some peace'. Young single parents on benefits or low income being particularly vulnerable to such pressure.

One teacher argued that some children miss out on normal child development because they spend much of their infancy in baby bouncers or strapped into cots, thus deprived of many hours of crawling and the attendant physiological, emotional and social development. Schools tried to compensate by providing equipment such as tunnels to crawl through and other motor-sensory experiences. Music, positive touching, yoga and peer massage were used in school as compensatory mechanisms as well as encouraging parents to work more closely with their children. Despite the current initiatives on healthy eating, in one inner city school half of the children came to school with packed lunches of chocolates and crisps, and in one case a child with seven chocolate bars as his lunch.

The prevalence and significance of such anecdotes is the contrast they present with teachers' accounts five years previously. Although, at that time, some teachers did refer to behavioural problems it was generally a reference to an insufficiently motivating curriculum for less able children. Revisiting the same schools, and often the same teachers, in 2007 there appeared to have been a significant and inimical impact on school life from a rapidly changing social scene. Motivating certain children, it was claimed, had become more difficult because by the time they come to school many of these children had become expert in manipulating adults.

Faced with deteriorating standards of behaviour and a growing tendency for some parents to take their child's side, primary schools have become more like their secondary counterparts in instituting formal recording systems whereby incidents are logged and behaviour monitored.

> We find everything we say we have to write down in a book... and although we always investigate every incident, you know, with some parents it's not enough. And so they will come in, you know, because the child will go home and say something's happened and, you know, children are children so how they say things isn't how it always actually happened so it's always investigated. Everything is written down, whether it's at lunchtime, mid-day or after school but you will still get some parents coming in demanding more. (Deputy Head teacher)

SENCOs (Special Educational Needs Co-ordinators), in particular, have seen their workload increase. In addition to increasing time given to parents (two hours with one parent on the day of the interview) 'an awful lot of time is spent resolving behavioural issues' in discussion with other professionals.

> Every other week I'll have meetings with behaviour support workers. We have triage meetings with two other SENCOs in the vicinity. The other agencies I'm involved in with the educational psychologist, half-term planning meetings and then meetings to do with any specific children. I'll have various meetings with various health professionals, the ones last week were with incontinence nurses. We've been trying to get social workers involved but it's not always easy, so we struggle with that a little bit.

Not all schools experienced the same level of difficulty. In one school with a diverse ethnic mix and an above average proportion of statemented children, and over 50 per cent of pupils in receipt of free school meals, behaviour was not an issue. This, it was claimed, was because of the generous staffing ratio (80 staff for 484 pupils) plus an an active parents' support group which helped to ameliorate the kinds of problems described above. The price to be paid for this was time spent in meetings with parents and in training the large number of TAs (35 out of the 80 staff) some of whom provided one-to-one support for pupils with the most complex learning needs.

The PPA revolution

The most constant theme running through all the teacher interviews was the liberation provided by PPA time, described as time for reflection, renewal and for planning. For teaching deputies and SENCOs with other responsibilities it was often used to as a time to catch up on urgent or outstanding tasks (completing a bid or following up on a child's case, for example). In most of the schools the arrangement consisted of having one afternoon during the week free of teaching commitments. Teachers were free either to stay in school or to work at home so that they could, should they wish, leave at noon. Most tend to stay in school to get access to resources, particularly web surfing where teachers often get ideas for lesson planning. It was also used for joint planning with colleagues teaching the same year group although there could be problems due to lack of suitable spaces to work.

> There have been some issues about working in school. We have been using the Deputy Head's room. I used to do it in the staff room but you have staff coming in and out and the odd child coming in. (Key Stage 1 teacher)

The main benefits of PPA time appear to come from teachers feeling valued and of having a greater sense of ownership over how and where they work.

> I go home [during PPA time] and it's absolutely terrific. I work on my own computer at home and I get far more done than if I was at school where you have children knocking on the door. (Key Stage 2 teacher)

However, in all but one school visited teachers said that having PPA time had not reduced the workload, although it had relieved the pressure by providing a period of concentrated time when something that needed doing urgently could be tackled. There appeared to be several reasons for this. First, the 'feel good' factor led some head teachers to develop new initiatives, designed to improve the curriculum or foster better relationships with the local community. For example, the head of the school with an above average number of children with special needs and diversity of ethnic backgrounds had previously allowed teachers planning time so that PPA had simply formalised an existing situation. As new cross-curricular activities had been introduced, in part due to the head's enthusiasm for SEAL (Social and Emotional Aspects of Learning), in part due to a major initiative designed to get 'reluctant' parents more involved in the school, teachers said the PPA time had just 'filled up'.

Similar sentiments were expressed in another school where joint planning was the norm and a number of new initiatives had been introduced.

> When it first started it [PPA time] was absolutely wonderful and last year when I didn't have planning meetings I was able to get a lot done. But now most of my time is taken up by planning meetings. (Year 3 teacher and member of SMT)

> PPA time is being squeezed because we are having much more put upon us and although it looks fantastic and it is fantastic... we are doing as much as we did before because we have more things to do, especially making resources for the new phonics programme. (Key Stage 1 teacher)

A further reason for any lack of reduction in workload was down to teachers themselves putting back into the day those things which they valued as part of a good 'all round' primary education. In our 2002 survey these had been cut out on account of the pressures of accountability and testing. While PPA bought time it was paid back with interest as teachers were now investing more time in events such as concerts and plays, and making more frequent outside visits. All required additional preparation time.

As PPA time takes place during lessons it means that planning is no longer done with the TAs present so that alternative times to share out the work need to be arranged. In general, PPA appeared to work better in schools with two form entry. Teachers working on their own in school were often 'fair game' when a crisis arose.

> I try to plan my PPA time but it's a bit of a struggle sometimes. If you end up at school you end up chatting to people and then you get roped in to doing something else, not intentionally or perhaps somebody been naughty in your class and whoever's in can't move them. (Year 2 teacher)

> Talking to other colleagues from other schools I think where it's a bigger school and there are parallel forms you've no alternative...but because you're a single class you've no shared time. (Year 6 teacher)

Much therefore depend on school leadership. In the school where teachers said workloads had decreased and that they often had left school by 4, the camaraderie and collegiality in the school had noticeably improved, a function of the support and mentoring which teachers get from colleagues. A pairing scheme had been instituted whereby more experienced teachers worked with those less experienced. The new head had drastically cut down on documentation and lightened the administrative burden on staff by taking on extra tasks within the senior management team.

It's still time consuming: It goes with the job

Undoubtedly, the most significant change since our previous survey has been the increase in the use of teaching assistants, partly as a result of the greater attention given to inclusion policies and partly as a way of coping with PPA time. In the 2002 survey most teachers strongly resisted the idea that classes should be taken over by non-qualified teaching staff.

> They talk about having a classroom assistant relieving you and having non-contact time. But then I see myself as a professional and I'm thinking how can a classroom assistant be left with a whole class? I don't see it's going to work. I've done the planning for this and I know what needs to be delivered. And I'd have to find time to talk to that classroom assistant to deliver that class. I wouldn't feel as if I'm in control somehow. [Teacher, 20 years' experience] (Galton and MacBeath, 2002:55)

Now most teachers were still unhappy at the idea of teaching assistants taking over their class, while others were concerned about the use of TAs as cheap labour.

> PPA time benefits me but it doesn't benefit the children. When there are specialists like the Italian teacher or the drumming lesson, that's OK but we leave easy work

for children to do when TAs are taking the class. (Key Stage 2 teacher: 8 years' experience)

Although PPA time is good I think they need to put more money in it so we can cover PPA time with teachers. I mean that's not getting at the HLTA because they do a very good job. (Deputy Head and Key Stage 2 teacher)

In all schools PPA time was covered by the use of a mixture of senior management and HLTAs (Higher Level Teaching Assistants). Generally, the top end of Key Stage 2, particularly the SAT year was protected and taken by other teachers, as one head teacher explained:

Well we've got three HLTAs. So in Foundation Stage, Year 1 and Year 2 it's been covered by HLTAs. In Year 3 depending on the cohort it's yes and no. It depends. Depends on the cohort. Year 4 go swimming so a TA has trained up and we send the TA, two TAs plus parent helpers and that works well. In Year 5 we've a part time teacher and we've paid her extra and in Year 6 I do it. So you can say broadly teachers in at Key Stage 2 and HLTAs lower down. (Head teacher, one form entry school)

Often head teachers were in no position to fix budgets until the very last moment because funding can vary from year to year depending on the size of the intake cohort and its composition. As the head quoted above explained:

It's a huge thing getting all these teachers out for half a day because we haven't had funding just to put a teacher in and it's depending on the cohort and the making up of the cohort. I can't just say you're a HLTA and that's your contract. And the workload for the bursar is absolutely phenomenal because she's filling in time sheets and taking them off this rate and putting them on that rate. We can't just issue a contract because it changes. It keeps changing. (Head teacher, one form entry school)

Reading between the lines there is a sense of head teachers having to do the best they can with limited resources and of teachers, while unhappy with these arrangements, being prepared to live with them because of the benefits accruing from PPA time. Teaching assistants are mostly valued for the help they can provide with small group teaching and in coping with particular children, although the consequences of this approach for SEN pupils themselves can be problematic. When TA time is concentrated on supporting children with special needs their capacity to take over many of the 24 clerical tasks is limited so teachers still find themselves congregating around the photocopies at 8.50 a.m. or at the end of the school day. Other teachers still took the time to put up their own displays.

Overall, there appeared to be less anger and disillusion among the primary teachers than we found back in 2002. Nobody now talked about 'getting out of teaching' although some with over 20 years' experience admitted to looking forward to retirement. The improved salary structure, PPA time and the consequent increase in the availability of support staff appeared to have given teachers a greater sense of confidence in their ability to cope. Most appeared to work the same or longer hours, with little reduction of time spent in the evening or at weekends. All, however, complained about the excessive paper work (particularly that associated with target setting) and having to cope with a continuing succession of new policy initiatives. Now, however, the prevailing spirit appears to be one resignation at these circumstances and an acceptance that the job of teaching will never return to a time when it was possible to chat informally with colleagues and where 'I would have gone off at a tangent … and talked about other things and they [pupils] would have drawn on their experiences' (Galton and MacBeath, 2002:40). Perhaps these sentiments are best summed up by one Year 6 teacher with ten years' experience.

> There are times when it's very frustrating, but then when you think. I can think there's a lot of us who have taught practically all the time and who can't think of anything else that you would do. It's either in one form, primary or adults you know, but that's… [pause] teaching you know.

> I can't see it being less. I think with the new strategy when it's more speaking and listening we may find that there's not much of a reduction. But for Year 6 you find some of it is quite… well still time consuming. But that's what you expect and you know that goes with the job.

 Questions for discussion

Is there now a generational gap between younger primary teachers and their more experienced colleagues? Do they share the same concerns, have the same priorities and adopt the same attitudes to recent reforms? What are the implications of any differences for future professional development?

Why do you think so many of the teachers interviewed still carried out many of the clerical tasks (for example, photocopying) which under the agreement were supposed to be done by non-teaching staff?

Is it legitimate for non-qualified staff to take charge of a class?

5

A Life in Secondary Teaching

This chapter discusses issues that arise for teachers in secondary schools in England. We begin with data from our survey in 2004 then revisit these issues in 2007 following Workforce Reform. Many of the issues of overriding concern – poor pupil behaviour, inclusion policies, curriculum overload, imposed targets, high stakes testing – were still in evidence three years on. While in 2007 teachers were happy to be relieved of some of the irksome and distracting tasks the essential dissatisfiers remained.

The secondary context

Our first report, *A Life in Teaching* gave us insights in to the life of primary staff, raising questions how these issues might play out in a secondary context. The secondary study followed a similar pattern to the primary study, comprising a survey followed by interviews with school staff and pupils. The survey gathered general information about teachers such as gender, age, years of teaching, responsibility position, subject specialism and type of school; the amount of time teachers spent on timetabled and non-timetabled work and the nature of that work; the amount of support teachers received in the class and extent of opportunities for collaboration with colleagues, for example, through cross-curricular activities; time given to record keeping, assessing pupils' work, formally testing pupils in class and in the lead up to external examinations; teachers' opinions on the impact of educational initiatives, and their effects pupils' educational experience and opportunities. There was also space for any further comments.

In interviews we followed up on the data from the survey, asking teachers about their working day and work done in evenings and weekends. Identifying a 'typical' day or week was more problematic than in the primary context but the interface between home and school, and the overflow between professional and personal lives resonated with the earlier study. We were also interested in pupils' perspectives and their understanding of what was involved in 'being a teacher'.

Our findings were derived from 216 surveys, nearly 50 hours of taped interviews, involving 40 teachers and approximately 60 pupils. Schools represented urban, suburban and rural settings, the smallest having 500 pupils the largest over 1,500.

Raising standards: Bought at a price

Our surveys took pace in a climate where raising standards had become an overriding concern of government, and indeed governments around the world. While teachers frequently commented on a rise in standards in their schools, this was seen as bought at a heavy price.

> Exam results have improved dramatically but nonetheless we are squashing them through and we are more and more successful and we look carefully at lessons to try and share good practice but we ask ourselves why? Why are doing this? Do these pupils really need to know these things we labour so hard to teach them? (Head of Humanities, 10 years' experience)

The support and good ideas within both National Curriculum and Key Stage 3 Strategies were welcomed but tempered by the reduction of freedom to teach inventively.

> There used to me much more freedom but having come as young member in just those years freedom to teach, opportunities to have that freedom, to make more exciting lessons have been cut and cut and cut as more and more prescription. I just don't feel that the lessons I am planning or the lesson I am planning for other teachers are necessarily the best, not the best for me not the best for the pupils. (Head of Humanities, 12 years' experience)

The most positive responses tended to come from less experienced teachers who welcomed the direction and practical guidance that the strategies offered them. It helped them survive in a challenging climate, echoing the comment of a teacher in the primary survey who said that the main advantage of the national strategies was that 'I don't have to think about what I am going to do.' Head teachers and teachers with longer experience expressed concern that newly qualified teachers had embraced the strategies 'like a security blanket', finding it difficult to conceive of the teaching in which they were required to think for themselves and devise their own strategies. There was a marked change in tone from a few years ago when NQTs were greeted with enthusiasm for the freshness of their thinking and seen as the lifeblood of the school.

More experienced teachers, however, were inclined to look beyond the imme-diate advantages of having a ready supply of material for lessons to consider the effects on pupils' motivation. Here, the research evidence supports their judgments in that pupils' attitudes towards the core subjects and liking for school has declined since the introduction of the Key Stage 3 strategies in Years 7 and 8 (Galton *et al.*, 2003). Interviews with pupils themselves supported these trends.

Initial teacher education and professional development

Initial teacher education and mentoring of newly qualified teachers was seen as an important step forward. Although generally applauded these were also seen as yet another set of pressures.

> In this school we try and protect young teachers, take the pressure off them, give them a lighter load, offer support where we can, take time out to observe and coach them. In a more ideal world that is precisely what they need, what we need, what the kids need. But in this world of non-stop hassle we don't feel we are doing justice to them or to the scheme. I'm afraid we may have to start turning down students too. It's a time issue. Nothing else. (Head of Science, 12 years' experience)

While CPD was also seen as a positive, in practice opportunities to attend courses were curtailed by the day-to-day imperatives of testing, Ofsted inspections, cover and the unforeseen crises that erupted without warning. As well as difficulties in attending courses there was also less time for the ongoing professional development within the school seen as the most valuable form:

> So much time is consumed with trivial things that little time is left for professional development. No adequate time for the real reflection. We can't talk with colleagues at leisure. There isn't that time. There isn't that professional space. But that's where you learn best, from each other, and when I think I am being disenfranchised from that I wonder about my role but people just say, well you have to just get on with it. (French teacher, 8 years' experience)

As the majority of professional development was taken up with national initiatives there was little room left for other forms of enterprise or inquiry, teachers' own interests or research projects. It meant that if teachers were to attend courses outside school permission would be granted for events that were practical, policy-related and with direct feedback into the subject department or school. The loss was, as one member of staff expressed it:

> We don't get the inspiration that comes from really challenging speakers and radical ideas that help us think outside the box and come back to school with a whole new way of thinking. (Geography teacher, 10 years' experience)

Factors that inhibit teaching

What did teachers consider to be the most serious obstacles affecting their work? We asked teachers to choose the five issues that they regarded as most seriously inhibiting of their ability to teach well, and to rank these issues in

Table 5.1 Most important obstacles to teaching in secondary schools

	SUM of rank for issue cited	Overall rank	Missing (or not in top 5)
Poor pupil behaviour	532	1	75
Lack of time for discussion and reflection	392	2	104
Large class sizes	351	3	127
Too many national initiatives	319	4	114
Overloaded curriculum content in own subject	253	5	146
Pressure to meet assessment targets	253	5	135
Poor resources, materials and equipment	229	7	145
Inclusion	187	8	156
Lack of parental support	180	9	156
Inadequate pay	142	10	173
Preparation for appraisal/inspection	129	11	174
Poorly maintained buildings	70	12	200
Prescribed methods of teaching	68	13	198
Limited professional opportunities	67	14	198
Insufficient pastoral support	29	15	210

order or seriousness. Limiting teachers to only five options gave us a clear priority order but did not imply that other factors with lower rankings were not also significant. In reading Table 5.1, therefore, it is important to bear in mind that the final column 'missing or not in top 5' means that teachers tended to cluster their responses in terms of what were seen as the key determining obstacles.

Examining these perceived obstacles whether by role and status of staff, or by years of experience, produced similar findings. Teachers with 25 years' plus experience, in common with teachers of less than five years' experience, ranked poor pupil behaviour as the most serious obstacle to teaching. However, much time was invested in planning there was always the possibility of the unforeseen incident or irritant that could sabotage a lesson. According to a Science AST with 15 years' experience it was 'a constant battle just to be allowed to teach'.

Behaviour: A matter of context

Poor pupil behaviour, ranked as the number one issue does not, as we have seen, exist in a vacuum. What was plainly evident from our field work in schools was the intrinsic relationship of behaviour to class size, inappropriate curriculum, pressure to meet targets and having to keep up with new initiatives, together with a lack of time for professional sharing and reflection. Where there were opportunities for professional development they often failed to address the issues most important to teachers or to provide the kind of accompanying support that would allow initiatives to take root. The impact of these issues were clearly evident to pupils:

> Teachers' attitudes are changing because nothing seems to stay the same for long. It's like there's a lot less time for you because there's lots of changes in one term or half-term, new teachers and teachers leaving, so that causes its own problems, discipline problems and learning because it is your relationship with the teacher that matters and you have to start building that all over again. (Girl, year 11)

Another pupil pointed out the ramifications of teachers' need to keep on top of things, strictness generating a blanket approach which ended in overreaction and unfair treatment.

> If they've got a really disruptive pupil they have to be really stern to just to keep one bad behaving pupil in line but not all pupils need that level of stern and then they suffer and they sometimes get it and get treated as if they're the problem pupil. (Girl, year 10)

Although ranked in eighth place, inclusion was integrally related to the other items. Teachers professed an inability to respond adequately to challenging behaviour without requisite resources, expertise and smaller class size. Dealing with the underlying causes of indiscipline rather than the immediate symptoms consumed time and energy. Problems were often deeply rooted and not amenable to a quick fix. Because teachers themselves were under so much pressure, issues were often left unresolved, and problems then resurfaced in other places. Teachers' frustrations not only arose from the growth in the number of such incidents, preventing them from fulfilling their main role as a subject specialist, but also from the increased administrative burden that such incidents imposed.

Lack of parental support

Although ranked ninth in order of priority, parental support was widely seen as a matter of concern. It was most acutely felt in relation to pupil attitudes and behaviour. Parents, it was said, were more likely to take umbrage, to support the pupil's version of events rather than side with the teachers, as would have been more common in the past. The nuclear and extended family were fast becoming a historical relic. Children and young people, it was said, were growing up in a new and challenging world, often bewildering to their teachers but it was teachers 'who bear the brunt', 'who are at the sharp end'.

> Parents do come in upset, angry, expressing a sense of injustice. If you take the time to listen, to be calm and hear them out they eventually confess that they are struggling with discipline. Their children are out of control. Their partners have

left. They can't pay the bills. They are fragile, volatile. (English teacher, 10 years' experience)

Few teachers resorted to blaming pupils or parents, tending frame the issues in terms of systemic factors, the most serious of which was lack of time to plan adequately, to tailor work appropriately to individual needs, to find appropriate support to deal with learning and behavioural difficulties, or to deal with students on an individual basis.

A life in the day of a teacher

We were able to gain a deeper and more rounded understanding of this by asking teachers to take us through a typical school day. The average school day of 6 hours and 48 minutes began with briefings, planning and preparation, breakfast clubs or other ad hoc meetings. The first hour in the morning was not a time for quiet preparation and planning. It was described as 'tense' because of unforeseeable crises.

> The first hour is very tense. It's very filled. And then we find out there's staff not in so we have to cover register and sometimes, if it's Monday there's an assembly to do. If I'm not doing that I'm seeing miscreants or I might even be doing good things (*laughs*) like handing out good conduct certificates. (Head of Upper School, 32 years' experience)

It then extended beyond school hours encompassing a wide rage of activities – meeting with pupils, counselling, preparation, marking, meetings, extra-curricular activities, study support, professional development activities. On average over a week teachers reported spending two and a half hours before the official start of school and nearly five hours a week after school. A further ten hours per week, again as an average figure, were spent on school work at home in evenings and weekends.

Teaching, learning and an overloaded curriculum

The overloaded curriculum ranked fifth in order of priority among obstacles to teaching. The picture we got of teaching in the year 2004 revealed only around a quarter of classroom time given to teacher whole class talk with about 60 per cent of the lesson spent in group or individual work. Teachers were asked to estimate the amount of time given to the following five categories:

- Talking to the class as a whole;
- Pupils working together co-operatively in groups or pairs, on work given by the teacher;
- Pupils working individually, at their own pace, on work given by the teacher;
- Pupils working on topics of their own choice;
- Other; please specify.

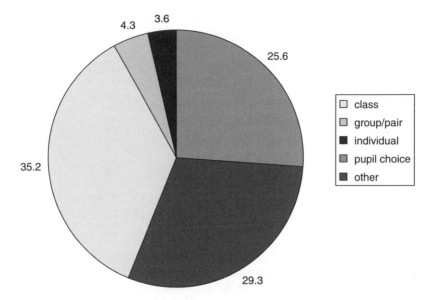

Figure 5.1 Percentage time used for teaching approaches

The distribution of mean times for teaching at Key Stage 3 (13–14 years old) is shown in Figure 5.1.

There was, however, a wide variation among teachers, even within the same subject area, in their teaching approaches. The 'other' category produced a list of 30 approaches including the following:

- Aural work;
- Class discussion/question/answer sessions/speaking and listening activities;
- Games;
- Thinking skills routines;
- Independent research (out of the class);
- Independent thinking, through starter activities;
- Long-term project research;
- One-to-one work with pupils on a rota;
- Pupils listening to tapes;
- Pupils presenting ideas to the class;
- Pupils teaching class;
- Role play, investigative/problem solving, exam technique;
- Teamwork;
- Video and audio presentations by the teacher;
- Whole class interactive whiteboard.

Cross-curricular activities appeared to be relatively rare. This is indicated by the very low response to this question, numbering under 30 out of a possible 216, the large majority answering 'none'. Examples of cross-curricular activity cited did, nonetheless illustrate some of the potential scope of this work. In total

82 examples were given, including cross-curricular themes such as numeracy, literacy, data handling and citizenship. There were examples of integration with the timetable being suspended for activity weeks, a 'One World Week', one-off days such as a 'Flexi Friday', a 'Zulu Day' integrating Music/Art/Dance and Year 6 to 7 transition schemes integrating English, Maths, Science and ICT, in addition to mainstream initiatives such as Vocational Education, work experience and Careers Days.

A sense of satisfaction in teaching?

Interviewees were unanimous as to what it was that gave them greatest satisfaction. In their different ways everyone said that on a good day it was the pupils' enjoyment of learning.

> The buzz you get when that little light goes on and it could be an understanding or it could be a piece of work that you think twice, 'Wow!' I think the biggest buzz I get is the learning. (AST English Teacher, 23 years' experience)

This was, however, seen as a less and less common occurrence in part due to 'excessive paper work and lack of time to finish anything properly', but also to a supervision (or 'snoopervision') climate.

> We are also much more observed and kept an eye on by senior staff and we in turn have to keep an eye on other people. Ever since Ofsted we are doing much more monitoring. (Curriculum manager, 10 years' experience)

While peer observation and mentoring were welcomed and performance management was of itself not seen as a problem, it was the straitjacket which monitoring imposed: a constant need to fit into a prescribed lesson format and the readiness to demonstrate that formulaic approach when the door opened to admit what was described as the 'policy police'. In practice, performance management tended to be seen as demoralising for teaching staff and in the opinion of senior managers, involved considerable amounts of extra work for what were seen as limited benefits.

Support for teaching

In what was generally described as an oppressive climate, teachers frequently mentioned a need for support. 'Support' is, however, a broad and ambiguous notion and a range of suggestions were offered:

- Assistance with lower ability groups;
- Behavioural support;
- Time to plan together with other staff;
- Support with special needs and/or able and talented;
- Planning courses;
- Assistance with ICT usage in class;

- Help in developing new teaching materials;
- Help in preparing resources and organising fieldwork;
- Smaller classes;
- Varying approaches and working with different learning styles.

The largest category by far was support for small group work (53.4 per cent of all responses to the questionnaire). What teachers wanted above all was to be able to offer informed and expert support to children struggling with understanding and with motivation. The priority was not simply for 'another pair of hands' but for someone qualified in special educational needs who could advise and provide the kind of high-level expertise required.

While teachers also mentioned routine irritants such as help with registers and attendance, chasing pupils about attendance or coursework, paperwork and report writing, it was primarily collegial and moral support that teachers most typically asked for. Support in its most profound sense referred to what teachers need emotionally, physically and intellectually to do the job that brought them into the profession and to gain the satisfaction and fulfilment that teaching can inspire.

This is the kind of support that is most acutely needed by newly qualified and less experienced teachers in their first years of practice. The need to be seen as strong, to keep on top of things, to convey an image of competence and control means a reluctance to admit to problems and ask for help. Nor is this simply a problem for inexperienced or newly qualified staff. Teachers with long experience were no less likely to talk about need for support in order to cope with the range of tasks they were expected to undertake in a climate of greater pressure, deteriorating pupil behaviour and constant teacher turnover. In one of our case study schools there was a turnover of 24 staff in the previous year rendering the existing support structure unsustainable.

Comments written by teachers on their questionnaire forms in 2004 had a poignant resonance.

> I have lived/taught through a period where we were respected as professionals and if asked we would do whatever was requested. Now heavy accountability has replaced this. I have excellent examination results, the pupils love my lessons and write to me after leaving describing what they ended up doing and thank me but I now hate the job and am considering leaving for a career in entomology. (Science teacher, 21 years' experience)

> I'm leaving the profession I love because I want my life back. It will break my heart to leave those kids but my family miss me! (Science Key Stage 3 Co-ordinator, 7 years' teaching experience)

And three years later in 2007:

> Will I stay? I think it depends on my mental health because I'm not willing to go back on that heavy medication. There are more important things in life. I don't know. I don't want to leave teaching.

> My mum's a teacher and when I said I want to be one she said 'Jesus are you alright?'

Life after workforce reform: Back to the future

Three years on and with Workforce Reform bedded down what has changed?

> Where should I start? I'll give you the same answer I gave last time. I work every minute of the day. I work through break, all through lunch. . . . One of the problems in English is the marking. Marking has always been the bane of English teachers' lives. There is no way I can do marking in school, things that are far more important have to be done in school so the marking goes home. I take work home most nights, these days I work at weekends as well. I do my preparation in the holidays.

The teachers' day and the teacher's week looks remarkably similar to 'BWR' (Before Workforce Reform).

> My teaching time has only gone down by two hours a fortnight and that's easily taken up by another meeting I have to have with the Deputy Head plus my 'emergency duty'. I'm expected to do so much more in the same time.

While in the primary context there was some evidence of teachers benefiting from PPA time, in the secondary context it appeared to make little difference.

> PPA time has made no difference. It has always been there. We have always had the space for planning and marking time but the difference now is that it is protected time, well at least in theory.

In practice:

> If you have allocated some time in the day to prepare the lessons and something kicks off then you just have to deal with that . . . or an irate parent coming in then you have to deal with that so when push come to shove the one thing that goes is the allocated time for preparation and marking. (Pastoral Head for Year 7/8)

Our evidence, while limited to these five secondary schools, suggests that if anything, the teaching day and week is now longer. Arriving at school by 7.30 a.m. and leaving after 5 p.m. was frequently cited as typical, at least by teachers in middle or senior management.

> Two to three nights a week there are meetings. Just before half-term I had four nights a week. After school is normally the time as well that I will see parents.

Unequivocally, for head teachers and senior leaders workload was now more onerous than three years previously. One head teacher, who described her working week as typical of other heads in her federation, said the following:

> A typical working day is from 7.30 until 6.45 when they kick me out. Three nights a week I don't get home until ten. In addition to eight governors' meetings there

are four confederation meetings plus parent meetings and other ad hoc events. (Head teacher, 10 years' experience)

Re-designation as a specialist school had added to the burden.

> It is hugely time consuming, phenomenal amount of time spent in trying to adjust to what they require in terms of development plans. The rhetoric is that you draw up your own plan but in reality you have to conform to their very strict template and then they send you back, and send you back again, to do it better, like a kid who hasn't done his homework properly, to do it over again properly.

There were similar complaints in relation to the SEF (Self Evaluation Form). Although it is not mandatory it was seen by heads as a high-risk strategy to depart from the required laborious and time-consuming format (MacBeath, 2006).

> Not mandatory? Filling it out stretched over two weekends, eight hours on each on Saturday and Sunday, over two weekends. This was my 'short' SEF. 60 pages long!

The 2006 Teachers Workload Survey (OME 2006) provides supporting quantitative evidence for these findings as to the pressures on senior managers. The small reduction in teachers' working hours from 51.3 in 2000 to 49.1 in 2006 has to be set against a rise in head teachers' hours over the same period from 60.8 to 65.1 and for deputies from 58.6 to 61.0.

Managing behaviour

It is in relation to behaviour management that Workforce Reform has perhaps had the most significant impact. It was described in one school as the major 'cultural shift', a structural division between teaching and pastoral care. 'We no longer pick up behaviour problems in the classroom', it was said by one teacher, relying on a new cadre of behavioural or pastoral staff to deal with miscreants.

However, this new layer of staff are generally described as 'managers', and while they may abstract children from the classroom, offer one-to-one guidance or impose sanctions, they tend not to see themselves as directly intervening in classrooms or as compensating for teachers' inability to contain problems (in some cases which teachers themselves have created). As one Pastoral Manager suggested:

> It will be difficult for some teachers to understand that our role is not picking up problems in the classroom but to have an overall leadership and management view of what is going on in the classroom.

Behavioural, pastoral and 'progress' managers are often in charge of 200 or 300 pupils. It is they who liaise with parents (although parents very often want to see the classroom teacher) while for their part teachers struggled to come to terms with the divorce between the personalised caring side of their relationships and 'teaching' as something purely academic.

> An awful amount of those roles are now academic mentoring and monitoring. It's still very much on attainment, and the other thing that really cracked me up last year... was being told that I wasn't going to have my form class, by e-mail at a weekend, and the kids that I'd taken care of for the past three years were going to be taken away from me.

There was also widespread concern that this new cadre of pastoral staff were very often unqualified, or at least staff without teaching qualifications, in some cases people who has come through the ranks from lunchtime supervisors to TAs and HLTAs.

> There are less people inclined to do the pastoral job because there is this perception that anyone could do the job. You don't have to be a teacher to do the job. There have been advertisements in the paper for a non-teaching person to do the job. It's giving people the perception that the pastoral role can be done by layman. (Pastoral Head Year 7/8)

Discipline policies too had taken on a new meaning in a climate of potential litigation and more complex home-school relationships. While schools are encouraged by DCSF to consult widely in drawing up their policies, departmental guidelines were seen as less than helpful.

> Devising the discipline policy was a nightmare. The DCSF guidelines are 67 pages. We sent out 1,526 letters two weeks ago, inviting e-mail or written responses. So far we have had one reply. We did get good advice from a consultant we bought in. He told us to keep our policy to broad principles, no detail, nothing too specific which you can't defend if you're facing a barrister. (Head teacher, 10 years' experience)

Heads and some teaching staff spoke of having to cover your back, with pupils and with parents but at the same time only seeing parents at times of sanctions and in a confrontative context.

> What annoys me and breaks my heart is when we've got students who will book parents appointments and come themselves because Mum and Dad can't or won't come and the kids will come in and ask you and say 'how have I done this year sir?' (Pastoral Head Years 8/9)

Still no pedagogy?

Despite Ofsted's *New Relationhip with Schools* (MacBeath, 2006) there remains a perception among teachers that teaching has to follow the formulaic three/four part lesson, remembering to put objectives on the board, while forgetting warm-up activities or failing to end with a plenary are cardinal sins.

Ofsted tells us what we need to be doing but says nothing about the bigger picture of a child's learning or a child's development. There are teachers who have brilliant relationships with students but because they won't do what Ofsted want them to do they get deemed as an unsatisfactory teacher. So yes there is much more of a drive towards goals, grades and not children's development.

Such a comment may do violence to inspectors who struggle to liberate teachers from the delivery straitjacket but it does reveal a widespread perception that teachers have no 'wiggle room', a perception reinforced when there are adverse experiences of inspection and a prevailing pressure not of teachers' own making.

At the end of the day you are judged by what kids get in the exam as a department or as an individual teacher. At the beginning of the year we get a sheet for your individual pupils and you have to explain why one of them is not making the threshold. You keep being told you've got to adapt to visual learners, kinaesthetic learners, blah-blah-blah and you start turning off BUT the kids are still judged in a two-hour exam.

This complaint is compounded by professional development that appears not to be concerned with pedagogy, bereft of discussion of what and how children are learning and teachers starved of time for collegial reflection.

Every single training day is chocka with new initiatives and people talking at us and there's no time for departments to sit down and talk about how things are going, how kids are getting on, if there's any problems, could we do this differently. It's all about we've got to get this done, we've got to get that done, we've got to get the other done – so there's no time for that sort of reflection.

Nor did interviews with young people give cause to contest the view that learning had been robbed of creativity and 'Eureka moments'. The following comment from an interviewer's notes tells a story that we found all too depressingly familiar.

Interviewer: What's the best thing you've done in this school? When you're as old as me what will you remember when you look back?

Comment: Dead silence! I was really struck by how unexcited they were by school. They had no Eureka moments, nothing really memorable, everything seemed really dull. They just wanted to get good grades so that they could get good jobs. They certainly weren't excited by learning (or that was the impression they gave me).

The fall and rise of managerialism

Our Head is a businessman – he's very good at what he does. I think he doesn't care as long as he gets what he wants. (Pastoral Head, Years 10/11)

While in rhetoric, and enshrined in the publications of the National College (NCSL), we have emerged from the dark era of managerialism into the enlightened age of leadership, Workload Reform seems to have driven schools backwards, at least in the secondary sector, to a business-like concern for efficiency rather than effectiveness, for delivery rather than growth, for executive decision-making rather than consultation. This may be a harsh judgement on the many inspirational leaders who keep alive an educational mission yet to do so requires not only a high human cost but, as Eliot Eisner put it, a vision and persisting commitment 'to swimming upstream'.

 ## Questions for discussion

Does Eisner's metaphor of 'swimming upstream' say something pertinent about teachers' experience in the last few years?

How would you explain the apparent slight decrease in teachers' workload in relation to the marked increase in the workloads of senior managers?

What does the word 'support' mean to you?

Has workforce reform driven school backwards to more hierarchical structures and accompanying workplace cultures?

The Inclusion Enigma: The Policy Context

In this chapter, we examine the context of our 2006 NUT-sponsored study into the impact of inclusion. The study took place at a time when the issues had been brought to the surface by Baroness Warnock's recant on her earlier embrace of mainstreaming for children with special needs. We briefly trace some of the history of legislation around pupils with 'handicap' and 'disability' and the paradoxes in trying to provide for children on an equal playing field within a market economy and high-stakes testing. We portray three worlds of inclusion of policy makers, academics and advocates, and the world of schools and classrooms.

The end of deficit and the dawn of integration

Pupils, no matter their particular needs or learning disabilities, belong together with their same age in the educational mainstream. This was the view of the landmark Warnock Report in 1978. Warnock's finding that 'one in five' pupils would experience learning difficulties at some point during their time at school challenged earlier assumptions that there existed group of pupils clearly distinguishable from the majority and requiring special help, preferably in special places. Three years later, the Education Act (1981) provided the impetus for the move towards integration of pupils with various forms of 'learning disability' into mainstream classrooms so that failure to learn would be down to the nature of instruction, construed as a task for all teachers and not just experts.

The 1981 Education Act abolished formal labels of handicap and instead required schools to determine the 'special educational needs' of all pupils and provide appropriate forms of instruction, much of it, given the numbers involved and the transient nature of some problems, in mainstream classrooms. The role of the expert within the school shifted. Instead of providing remedial tuition Special Educational Needs Co-ordinators (SENCOs) were to offer advice, support and training to their colleagues.

According to Ainscow and Muncey (1989:13) the notion that 'one in five' pupils might at one time or another experience problems with their learning too often was interpreted by schools as meaning that the bottom 20 per cent of pupils had special educational needs of one kind or another. However, far from abandoning labelling of a minority of pupils, many of the decisions about a child's ability to learn were made on the basis of inappropriate classroom behaviour rather than on needs or prior achievement (Croll and Moses, 1985 in relation to primary schools; Giles and Dunlop, 1989 in the secondary context).

The advent of the National Curriculum, however, emphasised the entitlement of all children to the same broad and balanced curriculum, while the 1994 Code of Practice, argued that there was a continuum of needs and provision and, as a consequence, most children should stay in mainstream schools regardless of whether or not there was a statutory assessment or statement. By 1996, Ofsted reported that most schools had set up relevant systems but that SENCOs were largely drawn from existing staff (and were thus untrained) and that there were considerable problems in adjusting the curriculum to match the needs of these pupils.

According to Tomlinson (2005) however, the *market forces* approach tended to cut across this attempt to develop a more equitable, coherent and humane policy for SEN pupils. Schools concerned with doing well in the exams league table did their best to avoid too many of these students, while other schools, deserted by middle-class parents because of their lower league position, took in additional numbers in order to claim the available resources in an effort to balance the budget and retain viable staffing levels (Tomlinson, 2005:81).

At the same time there is an apparent escalation of children with some form of physical, emotional or intellectual disability, ironically due to continuous advances in medical knowledge and accompanying technology which has offered children not only a life (which would have in previous generations been denied them) but also an enhanced quality of life. One consequence is, writes Tomlinson (2005:134), is a demand by knowledgeable middle-class parents for special segregated facilities, so concentrating limited resources on 'contemporary' disabilities such as autism, attention deficit hyperactivity disorder (ADHD) and dyslexia. The result, according to the Audit Commission (2002) is to divert Local Authorities designated funding, away from pupils with lesser levels of special educational need.

Wedell (2005) has argued that the continued emphasis on the 'standards agenda' and the assumption that this is best achieved through whole class teaching if maintained (p. 5) will fail to provide a context in which special educational needs can be effectively addressed. In 2004, Ofsted commented that the inflexibility of school and classroom organisation could sometimes be 'handicaps to effective developments'.

Studies reported in Chapters 3 and 4 had alerted us to some of the above dilemmas, in particular, pressure on SENCOs and support staff in coping with special learning needs against a background of deterioration in class-room behaviour and an increase in anti-school, anti-learning attitudes among pupils in general. It therefore seemed appropriate to conduct a further more detailed investigation of the issues surrounding teachers' attempts to implement 'inclusive' policies. Shortly after we began the study, Dame Mary Warnock confessed that the original committee in 1978 had made significant errors of judgement. The first error of judgment she argued, lay in seeking to remove the old system of categorising children. While the 1978 Committee had chosen to adopt the term 'Special Educational Needs', or SEN for short, as a generic description of all forms of learning disability, Warnock now concluded that:

> the idea of transforming talk of disability into talk of what children need has turned out to be a baneful one. If children's needs are to be assessed by public discussion and met by public expenditure it is absolutely necessary to have ways of identifying not only what is needed but also why (by virtue of what condition or disability) it is needed ... the failure to distinguish various kinds of need has been disastrous for many children. (ibid. 20)

Dame Mary's case was that the failure of the 1978 Committee to arrive at clearer definitions of need and to specify the requirements of different forms of learning disability, had saved successive governments from facing up to the true costs of resourcing the shift from special schools to mainstream education. Despite significant increase in government spending on special needs, in most schools there are now insufficient resources to cope with both range and complexity of special need.

The 1978 Warnock Committee's second error, 'possibly the most disastrous legacy' (p. 20) was the advocacy of an 'integrationist' approach within the framework laid down by the government of the day. The committee was told they should not count children whose mother tongue was not English or those living in particularly deprived circumstances among those having 'special needs'. In both cases, the reason was that language provision and family support was channelled through the Home Office and the Social Services respectively and the Department of Education did not wish to be saddled with this expenditure. As a result, the committee was not able to stress the links between social deprivation and learning disability nor to advocate additional resources for schools who found themselves having to cope with a sizeable proportion of such pupils with this double disadvantage.

Acknowledging that there is still a case for protecting children with acute learning problems, the 1978 committee recommended that such children should receive a statement of special need. What was not clear, however, was the criteria for 'statementing' pupils who had moved to mainstream education. In practice the number of statements issued during the next decade varied enormously from one Local Authorities to another. As the financial constraints hit LEAs during the 1990s, decisions about who to statement were decided on the basis of resources available rather than need. LEAs acted as both judge and jury in deciding parental appeals against decisions not to provide a statement of needs and, not surprisingly, tended to favour low costs solutions whenever possible. At the same time the deeper issue of statementing as rational form of funding and provision remained unaddressed.

Both the Audit Commission Report (2002) and Ofsted (2004) have confirmed the disparities and confusion in the current provision system, pointing to long delays in the statementing procedures with too many parents failing to get their applications for mainstream schooling accepted with wide variations from one local authority to the next. Special schools, it was claimed, were increasingly uncertain of their role. Ofsted also commented that the decline in classroom discipline, particularly in secondary schools, had led to an increase in the number of untrained classroom assistants whose main task was to contain poor behaviour. The discipline issue was a growing problem, creating a classroom environment in which the imperative of control made it more difficult for teachers to attend to individual needs.

Further evidence that all was not well with current practice emerged from a survey of SENCOs. This highlighted a shortage of professional support, especially from speech therapists and educational psychologists, and limited training opportunities due to budgetary cuts as the key factors placing severe constraints on a school's attempts to implement successful inclusion policies (NUT, 2003).

DfES statistics on school exclusions reported 10,000 permanent exclusions from primary, secondary and all special schools in 2003/04 representing 0.13 per cent of pupils (13 in every 10,000) (2004/05). In this year, there were just over 200,000 pupils who had one or more fixed period exclusions representing 2.6 per cent of the school population. By definition, pupils who face school exclusion are not 'included' and those who are permanently excluded are most likely to drop out of school altogether and are more likely than their peers to be found amongst the prison population in the future. The predominant reasons for both types of exclusion were persistent disruption, verbal abuse/threatening behaviour against an adult and physical assault against a pupil. Pupils with statements of SEN, the report found, were almost four times more likely to be excluded than the rest of the school population. The rate of exclusion also disproportionately penalises some ethnic groups, for example, the rate for Black Afro-Carribean pupils is 20 times higher than for Chinese or Indian pupils.

Faced with evidence such as this Warnock (2005) concluded that the policy of inclusion and the associated practice of issuing statements needs to be reviewed. She argued (p. 37) that inclusion should mean that all children 'should be included under the common educational project, not that they should be included under one roof', and points to the recent decision to set up specialist SEN schools as one possible way forward.

The three worlds of inclusion

The change of mind by Baroness Warnock re-ignited the debate and exposed three quite different 'worlds' of thought.

The first world is that of the policy maker. It is a world of fine intentions, one that makes bold claims and with high rhetoric, yet fails to follow through the consequences of the initiatives it espouses. Its purposes often conflict and good practice is often blind to context and the day-to-day realities of life in schools and classrooms. When schools are viewed as a microcosm of a truly democratic society they should, in principle, offer equal opportunities to all so that rewarding individuals according to their achievements can be seen as fair and reasonable. However, as Warnock (2005: 41) comments, it cannot be argued *a priori* that 'the values within a school must necessarily be identical to the values in a society of adults'. Furthermore, the failure to include social disadvantage or language deficiencies as components of an individual's 'special need' renders the ideal of 'equal opportunity' highly problematic.

In this, the policy maker's world, the raising standards agenda dominates the debate and frames the practice so that far from equalising opportunity it highlights and exacerbates differential achievement. In the US, where similar themes dominate the educational agenda, David Berliner (2006) describes a new view of children as 'grade enhancers or grade detractors', a constricting lens which shields us from their identities as children with all their own traits, abilities and unique personalities. Failing to make the grade carries far reaching consequences for all those involved, for schools in a competitive market, for teachers who are held accountable for their pupils' performance and for pupils whose self-esteem is commensurate with the level they are deemed to be at or aspiring to. A 2006 study by Libby found that carrying the label of a 4 or a 2 had a powerful impact on peer relationships, damaging to both high and low achievers.

While the policy embrace of *personalised learning* may seem to offer a more equal playing field, under the drive to raise standards, personalised learning may mean little more than increased diagnostic testing, tighter target setting and additional pre- and after-school booster classes. Together with the government embrace of *Assessment for Learning* we might expect to witness a shift in pedagogy. 'Deep learning' (Entwistle, 1987), implicit in assessment for learning, does, however, sit uneasily with key stage testing and the need to meet the diversity of needs that a genuinely inclusive approach would imply.

The second world of inclusion

The second world is the world of aspirational classroom practice. It belongs to those who envisage a real potential of the classroom as learning arena for all. Its proponents argue that the pedagogy employed by the most effective teachers of children with special needs differs little from the research-based frameworks developed for use in mainstream teaching. It implies a reforming agenda which requires changes not only in the way that teachers help children engage with the curriculum but also in the way the curriculum itself is shaped and constructed (Lewis and Norwich, 2005). This is a world in which the inclusion of large numbers of SEN pupils in mainstream classrooms is seen not as a problem but as an opportunity – a potential solution to current difficulties that have seen year-by-year dips in the attitudes of pupils in primary and lower secondary school and a decline in levels of discipline (Galton *et al.*, 2002). Underpinning this is a view of inclusion as a basic human right by virtue of Article 26 of the United Nations Universal Declaration of Human Rights, interpreted to mean inclusion within a mainstream school, since it is also a right of parents to choose a mainstream school for their child. Under the 2002 Special Needs and Disability Act, school governors and head teachers may be at risk of prosecution if they refuse a school place to children with special educational needs, even if the school does not have sufficient resources to provide an appropriate curriculum.

It is not unreasonable to claim that existing pedagogy contributes to the present problems of poor motivation and low disposition to learn found even among more able pupils. Many teachers would appear to acknowledge this and agree that teaching methods need to be revised to allow greater pupil participation and less teacher direction. However, it is a mistake to believe that because of the strength of the argument for a radical overhaul of practice that change will necessarily follow. Change has a complex history and an uncertain future. Effective pedagogy may be effective pedagogy no matter the clientele but this it to ignore the regulatory power of government and the mechanisms which shape and control pedagogy (curriculum, assessment, inspection and school organisation, for example).

Thus it is that in England the nineteenth-century received view of elementary education, which was grounded in the teaching of the '3Rs' still dominates 'the core curriculum' despite the fact that cultural and social plurality of today's primary classroom is at odds with the main purpose of the elementary curriculum, which was to contain the masses rather than liberate them (Alexander, 1995: 56–66). As a result an open child-centred pedagogy may be no freer from these external culturally determined controls than traditional didactic instruction, because both are constrained through the mechanisms of differentiation and assessment.

A third world view of inclusion?

So the third view of the world in which we can explore the meaning of inclusion is that of the classroom as it exists today rather than it might exist in the future. It is not the policy maker's world, the world of the academic or the committed advocate but the world of the classroom teacher. Nor do teachers even live in the same world as their senior leaders who are required to make decisions often based on compliance and expediency and relevant as much to the world beyond the school walls as to the world within it. It is teachers who are at the sharp end of policies which they have had no hand in framing and who typically bend their will to someone's agenda with surprising tenacity, and sometimes achieve a measure of success against the odds.

It is, however, a world in which success is unpredictable. It is a world in which things may change from day to day because teachers are not in control of admissions policy, of staffing, of changing government priorities or local authority decisions. Nor do they have a say in housing policies, employment, immigration and migration or the 101 forms of 'incentivisation' in the bidding-led educational economy.

It is this third world that was the arena for our study in 2004/05, but one nested within both the first and second worlds. Like Eliot Eisner (2005) we might set out to find a pedagogy which embraces surprise, discovers outcomes and creates classrooms that are interesting rather than tidy, but as he writes, we cannot lose sight of the connections between the micro methodology of the classroom, and the macro methodology of policy and ideology.

> ...decisions about method are not simply decisions about method. They are also political decisions that have to do with who is competent and who is not, who is powerful and who is weak, who is skilled and who is unskilled, who does work that is relevant and who does not. (p. 4)

The inclusion study

Commissioned by the NUT to examine the impact of inclusion policies we came to the study through an understanding of where these three worlds collide, or meet. We did not begin either by endorsing or rejecting Baroness Warnock's critique but we were influenced by the strong views we had encountered in the previous two studies of primary and secondary. By the time those studies had both been completed there had been a noticeable increase in the use of support staff, very often assuming responsibilities that exceeded their remit or level of relevant expertise. Recommendations to the Government by the PricewaterhouseCoopers' study for an increase in support staff was especially relevant for children with special needs had raised anxieties among the teaching profession that this would result in untrained staff substituting for teachers in the classroom. Such anxieties have not been allayed but rather exacerbated by practices which, we found, had been gradually extending the scope of teaching assistants and other support staff.

These findings were significant in shaping our study, leading us to explore in greater depth the changing roles of teachers and support staff working in special needs within the present performance dominated policy culture. Of particular concern was the impact on pupils experiencing learning difficulties as well as on the nature of teaching and learning more generally. In these circumstances, it seemed more appropriate to explore participants' views in some depth through a series of interviews with key personnel in a selected number of case schools rather than using questionnaires complemented by interviews as in our two previous studies.

While review of the literature and data from the two prior studies were influential in shaping the nature of the inquiry, our work was set within a Faculty of Education with its highly respected special needs/inclusion team. We also brought to the study, therefore, an acute awareness of the case for inclusion and the advocacy for the cause among colleagues able to point to examples of successful inclusive practice. Achieving a balanced view required taking cognizance of that collective expertise while listening carefully and as objectively as possible to the viewpoints of teachers, parents and pupils.

The sample

In all, 20 schools were visited (10 first, middle primary; and 9 secondary and 2 special) from seven different LAs, chosen to represent a range of policies on inclusion though our study did not cover any with the highest numbers of pupils in Special Needs Schools. From those chosen, two were from the 20 LAs with the lowest proportion of all pupils in special schools and three were from the 20 LAs with the least numbers of pupils with statements in special schools using the available data in Local Authorities Inclusion Trends as a source. LAs were also chosen to represent a reasonable geographical spread and range of type: 1 in Inner London, 1 in Outer London, 1 Metropolitan and 4 County.

Thus in choosing schools a further objective was to provide a mix between rural and urban catchment areas, with the former likely to have mixed and fairly representative intakes whereas, in the latter areas, schools with disadvantaged populations were likely to have higher levels of pupils on the SEN register (see for example Dyson, 2004). Local authorities were sent a short questionnaire probing the nature of inclusion within the authority, and asking them to nominate up to five schools which they regarded as attempting, in one form or another, to implement a policy of inclusion. For primary schools the highest inclusion ratings were given to schools where pupils on the SEN register were:

- Included in most lessons in homogeneous groups;
- Supported mainly by trained teacher or assistant;

- Fully integrated into social/cultural activities;
- Linked with special schools and/or external support.

While the secondary schools were rated highly if they:

- Included SEN pupils in most lessons with specialist help available;
- Made a clear distinction between physical, learning and behavioural needs;
- Had shared social/cultural activities;
- Had close links with special and primary schools catering for special needs pupils.

In contrast to schools where SEN pupils

- Had a special curriculum distinct from that of mainstream classes;
- Were often placed in on-site units for pupils with physical / learning and / or behavioural needs.

Typically in each school between five and ten teachers were interviewed, likewise five to ten pupils and up to eight parents, the SENCO and the head teacher. Observations in classrooms were ad hoc by invitation but in some cases where there were two researchers in a school or a visit stretched over two days there were extended opportunities for observation in classrooms, gymnasia, special units and informal discussion in staff rooms and lunch rooms.

As a check against the extent to which the views expressed by the sample of teachers interviewed were representative of the school as a whole, a short questionnaire based on the interview questions was left with the SENCO or member of the senior management team with an invitation for other members of staff who were not interviewed to fill in and return these in the envelopes provided. In all 110 questionnaires were returned and were used to supplement the data obtained at interview. In summary, we deliberately set out to select schools that had made a commitment to implementing a policy of inclusion rather than selecting some schools that were not so involved. Our aim was to review current practice in favourable circumstances and not attempt to portray what was happening across the entire range. Where our research identifies problems and difficulties for children with learning difficulties, these issues are likely to be exacerbated elsewhere within the educational system in schools where inclusion is given a lower priority.

 Questions for discussion

Is there a case for including all children with special needs in mainstream classrooms?

Continued

Continued

When is inclusion not inclusion?

Who benefits most from including children with special needs in main-stream classrooms – Children themselves because there are both social and academic gains? Children in general because it is socially educative and broadens their horizons? Teachers, because it improves their pedagogy?

7

The Inclusion Enigma Findings and Implications of the Study

This chapter explores the third world of inclusion, the world inhabited by teachers struggling to provide the best for children and young people against the odds. It is a story of goodwill and professional endeavour but one deprived of two key fundamentals – resourcing and expertise. It is a story of overstretched teachers unable to cope with many of the demands placed on them. As our 2006 study showed, these inclusion strategies were often no more than containment and TAs found themselves taking on roles beyond their levels of confidence or competence.

The theory and practice of inclusion

The continuing trend to greater inclusion within mainstream classrooms has been welcomed in principle by teachers. It was widely agreed by teachers in our study that exclusion of certain children from the mainstream of school, social and academic life could not only harm them but also render them invisible to other children, so depriving them of important facets of a social and political education. However, the realities of inclusive practice took very differents and often take highly problematic forms, in summary:

- The nature of special needs which demand a more differentiated form of provision than containment within the mainstream classroom;
- The decision-making process whereby pupils are allocated to a school and to a teacher without adequate consultation and planning;
- Lack of expertise to deal with certain kinds of behavioural and learning needs;
- The nature and quality of support available;

- The impact on the balance of the teacher's work;
- The impact on all children's learning.

These issues do not stand in isolation from the policy context in which they are located. Nor do they play out in similar ways in different neighbourhoods, highly disparate socio-economic areas, local authorities with varied policies or in small and large primary and secondary schools located in rural areas or clustered together in inner cities or suburbs. In other words, the issues are context sensitive and return insistently to two key issues – resourcing and expertise.

These two key elements in the equation have to be seen in conjunction with the curriculum and testing, both of which drive teachers' time and motivation and place heavy constraints on what they are able to do to meet a range of disparate needs. As McLaughlin *et al.* (2005) have argued, it is the tensions between the two agendas – standards and needs – and the pressure exerted on teachers to meet curriculum targets, that play a part in shaping attitudes to special needs, not only those of school staff but of parents and pupils too.

Isolation, containment or support?

We found scant evidence of young people with special needs coping successfully within mainstream classrooms without some form of withdrawal, individualised or group support. Most secondary schools and even some junior/middle schools have some form of special unit, taking differing forms such as Learning Support Units, Seclusion or Isolation Units, Pupil Services Centres, all serving the function of support and/or containment and/or isolation.

The lowest common denominator was 'isolation', a place to send children who were disruptive, 'so that teachers can get on with teaching'. In two secondary schools visited there were Isolation Units for bad behaviour, explicitly set up as an alternative to exclusion. Since their inception the number of exclusions in both schools had gone down but it was typically special needs young people who ended up in these units and the expedient response to 'bad behaviour' did not necessarily discriminate among causal factors such as routine 'naughtiness' or a cry for help.

Visits to special units in schools often suggested more of a containment function, with TAs keeping young people engaged or amused with games, drawing, colouring in or worksheets designed to provide a differentiated version of class work, and sometimes engaged in the kind of tedious tasks that had sparked their behavioural protest in the first instance. These units also attempted to provide some form of counseling and 'talking through' the problems that had resulted in the pupil being placed there. In only a few schools, however, did we find a systematic and structured programme designed to meet individual learning needs by a flexible approach to differentiated provision.

Case Study Context: The class policeman

James is the class 'policeman'. He is acutely aware of right and wrong and frequently reprimands his peers when he disapproves of their behaviour. He is able to work in a group but his classmates get frustrated with his bossiness and sometimes groan when they discover he is to be in their group. Although he takes part in team sports he gets very upset when he perceives people to be breaking the rules and will sometimes stop the game to demand an explanation, or constantly point out things to the referee. He is also very intolerant of teachers who break their promises, are inconsistent or don't carry out threats. When he points out pupil misbehaviour to the teacher he gets into trouble with his peers for 'telling tales'.

The role and impact of learning support staff

Containment and curricular differentiation were two of the roles exercised by TAs. While their role varies widely from local authority to local authority and from school to school, in whatever capacity they operate they are indispensable to making inclusion work. At the same time this is problematic as they frequently assume responsibilities which exceed their expertise. This can often be put down to goodwill on their part, their concern for children in their care, but it is a responsibility assumed in default of better resourcing and other systemic issues which starve schools of requisite professional expertise and expect inclusion to be delivered on the cheap.

Typically an LSA will work on a one-to-one basis with a child, so playing a critical role in allowing teachers to attend to the rest of the class, releasing them from attending closely and responsively to that child's needs. When questioned about individual children, teachers often referred us to the LSA as they themselves had little contact with, or knowledge of, the children in question. They had neither the time to prepare appropriate materials for the child in question nor time for consultation with LSAs which would have allowed the latter to prepare materials under teachers' direction. However, teachers themselves often lacked the requisite expertise to be able to provide professional advice to their LSAs, so reinforcing the situation in which the teacher dealt with mainstream pupils while the LSA attended as best s/he could with the needs of the 'special' pupils.

A deputy head in a special school described TAs as 'mums', not in a dismissive way but with deep respect for the caring and mothering role they played. Yet, with all the goodwill and unpaid extra time they put into the job they could not offer the high level of specialist expertise required to support complex learning needs. Often their 'mothering' could be overprotective, creating dependency rather than independence, as it took acute judgment and experience to know when to challenge and encourage risk taking. Heads often spoke in glowing terms of TAs who had a natural instinct for working with young people but TAs themselves were the first to admit that they were carers rather than pedagogues. While there were instances of very expert TAs who bought with them a background of work in health, social services or education this was more the exception than the rule. There were mothers (and very occasionally fathers) of children with special needs, and while this could be very valuable it could also be problematic. First-hand knowledge of a Down's or autistic child could, on the one hand, inform and guide teachers' practice but could also mislead, either because the experience of individual cases was not generalisable or because the parent in question did not have the breadth of expertise in the education of their own child.

It was common to find LSAs taking responsibility for differentiating the curriculum, typically voluntarily and in their own time. In some schools an LSA in charge of a child would take home the lesson planned for the following day and devise a simplified version of the lesson. While such planning was, in some instances, informed by consultation with the class teacher, heavy workloads meant that it was often left to LSAs to manage differentiation of learning on their own. This was commented on in the 2002 Annual Ofsted report:

> ...pupils with SEN depended on teaching assistants to break the tasks down further so that they could participate. In these lessons the focus of the teachers' planning was on how the pupils with SEN could be kept engaged, rather than on what the pupils needed to learn next. There was not enough stress on how to improve their understanding and skills. This was a common reason why a significant number of pupils with SEN made too little progress, despite good teaching for the majority of the class. (Ofsted, 2002a, paragraph 72)

With direct reference to the Ofsted findings a secondary head commented:

> One reason for this is the inexorable pressure of the curriculum, examination/ SATs requirements and league tables which demand that mainstream teachers drive forward in a way that may not be conducive to good inclusive practice.

Special needs co-ordinators (SENCOs) might have been expected to exert a key role in provision but this was also problematic. In practice, their role appeared to be largely administrative, consisting of co-ordinating arrangements for deploying support staff, meeting with individual teachers, pupils and parents and liaising with outside professional bodies. Part of their reluctance to develop a curriculum co-ordinator role may also lie in their background. A minority of SENCOs in this study had a qualification in some aspect of supporting children with special learning needs. Because such posts are viewed, particularly in secondary schools, as carrying a high administrative burden they are often offered to staff whose qualifications are in areas which carry less 'academic prestige'.

The balance of teachers' work

Increasing the range of needs and abilities within the 'mainstream' classroom without addressing curriculum, testing and 'standards'-driven accountability, has had a major impact on the nature and balance of teachers' work. Within these policy parameters attempts to meet complex individual needs with a weather eye on overall standards, frequently upset the balance and flow of teaching and learning. A primary teacher referring to an autistic pupil said, 'My main focus for each day was him.' How to deal with this one child had, for her, become a constant preoccupation in the planning and in anticipation of the day ahead. She did not say this to blame the child or devalue the potential benefits to him of being in the company of his peers, but because the lack of support was beginning to drain the energy and motivation she had once brought to her teaching.

This was to prove a consistent theme in interviews and in written comments from school staff. Teachers and TAs who spoke about serious dislocation of teaching were not referring to special needs in general but to specific kinds of behaviour that were particularly disruptive, not only disturbing to others but causing teachers to worry about the child putting herself at risk.

> The thing that I can't handle and just have no clue what to do with is the self-harm, sometimes serious, like kids obsessively banging their head on the desk or on the wall. I find it deeply distressing. (Year 3 Teacher)

A group of primary teachers described an autistic boy who has just come in from nursery, describing him as 'physical', a reference to aggressive behaviour such as biting or kicking. They had worked hard to accommodate that behaviour but confessed to a lack of knowledge about autism, feeling both helpless and deskilled. There was only one teacher in the school trained in 'positive handling' and every time a child needed to be restrained this teacher had to go out of the class, leaving the TA with the rest of the pupils. The TA had eventually quit her job as she was unprepared to take the whole class. This group of highly committed teachers said that it had also 'taken its toll on staff' and some had left, unable to deal with the pressures of curriculum and testing on the one hand and the demands of 'difficult' children on the other.

These may be examples of more extreme cases but reflect concerns expressed by the National Autistic Society (NAS). Their 2002 survey *Inclusion and Autism: is it working?* found that children with autism and Asperger's syndrome were on average 20 times more likely to be excluded from school than their peers. One in five (21 per cent) were excluded at least once, compared with an estimated 1.2 per cent of the total pupil population. The situation was worse still for more able children with autism. Twenty-nine per cent have been excluded from school at one time or another. The study also found that three-quarters of schools were dissatisfied with the extent of training in autism. This is not to argue that there is not a place for autistic children within the mainstream, indeed there were examples of autistic children doing very well by virtue of their ability to focus exclusively to the task at hand and sensitive handling by teachers. Inclusion of particular kinds of needs does, however, have to address the ability of the school to provide the right environment and support for learning. In the absence of these conditions, as one teacher admitted: 'We don't do anything about their learning but at least we can help them to feel accepted by their peers.' It was, as another teacher put it, 'inclusion without education'.

For many children with specific medical needs a mainstream classroom was the best place to be and for many of these children special schools would not have been in their interest. However, we also found many extreme cases where medical conditions put huge strains on teachers and teaching assistants, for example, constant vigilance to ensure administration of tracheotomy at regular intervals, coping with incontinence and frequent nappy changing or clearing up after accidents. This made for a constant level of strain on the classroom teacher and a heightened sense of responsibility. As one primary teacher commented:

> Our planning takes so much longer – teachers have to ensure that there are always two people there at all times in case a child requires medical intervention, such as sucking out the tube or for a child who blacks out. [Jill wears a nappy and blacks out; Alistair requires suction for his tracheotomy tube.]

These are, again, relatively rare scenarios and more familiar to teachers in special schools, but even in that context, a special school Deputy Head said that teachers or TAs could not, and should not, be required to take on such responsibilities, and that all too often schools rely on the goodwill of staff and their instinctive sense of care for children. He described this as both unfair and exploitative. As one primary teacher commented 'we can accommodate some medical problems – but some are so severe you can't access the curriculum. It's more like nursing rather than education.'

 Case Study Context: Picking up social cues

Albert does not pick up on social cues and has few social graces. He has a very ironic sense of humour which is often interpreted as rudeness. He reacts very badly when he perceives something to be unfair and any displeasure or punishment he sees as rejection, withdrawing into himself and refusing to communicate. When he understands very clearly what is expected of him he will comply as long as he sees it is a reasonable request. The problem is that he gets into trouble quite a lot because his classmates' favourite sport is winding him up and then watching the fallout.

Meeting the needs of children on the borderline

It is the more dramatic cases such as these that grab the headlines and can easily misrepresent the larger issues. However, the issues often lie in the less manifest cases where children's learning is short-changed and teachers struggle to meet their needs. These are children on the borderline, sometimes quiet and withdrawn, sometimes demanding, not statemented or necessarily waiting for statementing. These children have not qualified for the support of an LSA and it was these children who could sometimes prove the most difficult for teachers to deal with.

> The children who are diagnosed or have been specified as needing a Strategic Facility, then they get their hours and their time but those children who don't quite make the bracket, they have a need but they don't have a strong enough need, they are the ones that really have to watch out or they just slip through the net. (Year 1 teacher)

It is in this borderland that children could 'slip through' causing no overt problems and easy to ignore in favour of attending to more demanding forms of behaviour. Others of those 'borderline' children could express their need or disaffection through disruptive behaviour which could escalate when there was a potent mix of children with behavioural special needs along with others to whom the wider levels of tolerance gave license to act up, especially during the temporary distraction of the teacher.

> Where it doesn't help is where you have a child that has behavioural difficulties and you have a mainstream child who also has behavioural difficulties and they play off one another, they copy, they learn tricks off each other, and then you have negative behaviours that you need to break – that's probably where it's not quite so easy. (Year 1 teacher)

A primary teacher exemplified this issue 'in extremis' with the case of a child with Tourette's syndrome whose uncontrollable interruptions had a knock-on effect with other children who took this both as a welcome distraction and an occasion for mischief. Children can get used to extreme behaviour and learn to ignore it. Learning to live with, and to understand, differing forms of behaviour as an expression of underlying needs is a significant aspect of social education. It may be regarded as a singular strength of inclusion policies.

> The year I had an autistic child – there was a lot of disruption – screaming. The other children just ignored it. They knew him from reception – so that may make a difference. When he was having a 'do' – the other children would just work around it. (Year 2 teacher)

Not all classrooms, however, are so accommodating. For some pupils and teachers such extreme forms of acting out proved both stressful and inimical to their concentration and focus on learning. It can take considerable time and a particular combination of circumstances for pupils to get used to unconventional and extreme forms of behaviour. Coming new to it in a secondary school context, as compared to learning to live with and adjust to it over a period of time in a primary school, was where the most acute issues surfaced. Behavioural and learning problems were exacerbated when a teacher was off ill and a supply teacher had to cover the class without the requisite knowledge, expertise or support.

This had repercussions on teachers who described having to 'pick up the pieces' after a period of inadequate cover. In some cases, teachers' concerns caused them to return too soon after an illness or made them reluctant to 'sell children short' by taking time off. Speaking of her staff a primary head described teachers 'as their own worst enemy' because of 'always putting the child before themselves'. A teacher spoke of the guilt she felt at letting children down.

> I think, it's a funny thing to say, I think they (SEN children) add guilt to my job. I go home sometimes and feel I haven't done a good job because I haven't given them enough time and I think it's because the progress they make is so slow that you can think that you're failing. (Reception teacher)

A very experienced primary school teacher, who constantly strived to frame the issues in positive terms, spoke emotionally about the sense of guilt and failure.

> We were doing something in Maths last week and they still hadn't got it and I felt a failure in myself. I got so emotional and I said to my TA because I was close to tears 'I've got to go out of the classroom'. I felt it was something I was failing in – I couldn't cope with it any more.

For teachers 'muddling through' without expert support, having to carry the burden of responsibility for children's welfare could weigh heavily. Success with challenging behaviour and complex needs is a long-term investment and highly gratifying when it finally pays off. However, as a special needs assistant pointed out, you may have to go through 'hell' to get there. 'He stayed in the school for three years and we saw him change – it was just hell for the first year.'

 ## Case Study Context: A matter of concentration

Joshua has a very short concentration and short-term memory span which means he gets easily distracted, can be very restless and very little of what he is taught is retained. This is particularly acute at end of terms and coming back to school after holidays. He never remembers to do homework or to bring what he needs for class, and messages home never arrive or are distorted en route. Although notes home are sometimes pinned to homework diaries they never seem to arrive. His mother frequently complains about lack of communication from the school, about stories Joshua has told her about never doing any work. She worries that Joshua is constantly in trouble for his 'bad', 'lazy' or forgetful behaviour and feels that her son's needs simply aren't being met.

Transitions

A common theme among primary staff was that secondary school could not offer the continuity of care offered in the primary. The issue tended to be expressed as a structural one – of size, impersonality, fragmentation of the school day and inflexibility of secondary curriculum. Over the course of six years in the primary school it was possible to build a culture and procedures which were well known to all staff, with norms and limits of tolerance that had been tested and established over time. In secondary it was, for children with special needs, a matter of starting anew, new faces among peers and teachers, and a wider variance in tolerance of staff for disruptive or demanding children. The years of work in primary, over a six-year period, could be undone before the child had a chance to accommodate to new surroundings.

> We've spent all this time and money and hours keeping them in here since reception and then you find out that they have been expelled within a couple of weeks (of going to secondary school). (Primary teacher)

A number of primary heads spoke of the long journey to build self-esteem among children who were conscious of being 'different', investing time and effort to help them feel accepted and valued, building self-esteem to then to see it vanish within a week or two.

From a secondary viewpoint some teachers and head teachers expressed the view that children arrived unprepared for the independence and resilience that a secondary school required. Trying to create the kind of close and caring 'family' environment of the primary school was seen as impossible to replicate. While strong and consistent communication between primary and secondary schools was of paramount importance, this could not itself guarantee that a disturbed or 'damaged' child would survive in what, from its point of view, might be a hostile and dangerous environment.

Yet, as many primary teachers and parents were quick to acknowledge, there were secondary schools that, in spite of the difficulties, coped well with the challenges of special needs. A number of essential factors were mentioned by primary and secondary staff – appropriate resourcing, a carefully studied admissions' policy, planning, a requisite range of expertise, accompanying professional development and a collaboration between primary and secondary grounded in good faith, good will, anticipation of potential problems and a commitment to proceed with hope and optimism.

As well as coping with the transition from one phase of schooling to another, children and young people with special needs are liable to experience more lateral movement from school to school. This is often a matter of trial and error as their parents try to find a school in which their children can be happy and in which school staff are struggling to achieve that desired state. A primary head teacher talked about neighbouring schools admitting to 'not having a clue what to do with children with complex needs'. She cited the case of a nine-year-old boy who became 'mentally ill' by being in a class where he just couldn't cope and the class teacher admitted to being 'totally out of her depth'.

A primary head talked about problem behaviour as prevalent among pupils who had come from other schools compared with pupils who had been in the school from reception onwards.

> If they come in from elsewhere they struggle. The special needs' kids progress well if they've had the reception teacher in this school and had the continuity of care.

The continuity of care, of expertise gained over time, was a constant theme in those primary schools which coped relatively well with special needs. They stressed the importance of reception as laying the foundations. One primary school head with expert Infant teachers complained that Key Stage 1 scores were so high that the school was not able to show added value thereafter. This was mentioned to emphasise the importance of those early years in a number of critical dimensions:

- Children's eagerness to learn and to be accepted;
- The willingness of children at that age to accept 'difference';
- The power of the first teacher to create an inclusive environment;
- The opportunity to maintain a broad and balanced curriculum.

Children who did not have that positive early advantage and had been shuttled from one school to another could be so damaged by the disconnected experience that appropriate placement could prove to be too little and too late.

> We had a little boy. We had him until Year 2 and then the Authority couldn't place him anywhere so we had him in Year 3 and then the Authority still couldn't place him so we had him until January as a Year 4. And we knew we weren't doing anything for him – we couldn't meet his needs. He went to residential and that didn't work out either. (Primary school, SENCO)

There seems to be a growing number of children involved in split placements where children's time is divided between the special school and their local mainstream school. Although this addresses parents' concerns about their children getting to know other children in their local community, this lack of continuity was an additional strain on those least equipped to deal with it. At secondary level this is often problematic in terms of timetabling and can mean that the pupil does not 'fit' anywhere and misses out in both schools. These issues play out in more acute forms in secondary schools. Teachers who see pupils for only one or two periods in the week have to get to know them, assess their needs and manage curriculum targets, spoke of the rapid transitions from one period to the next as bewildering for children with special needs settling in. Coping with the fragmented school day, the secondary curriculum and the period structure was too much for many young people who found themselves excluded within the first few weeks of secondary school.

Case Study Context: Eager to please

Amelia is a keen learner in class. Her teachers describe her as bright, keen to join in, always with her hand up, desperately eager to please. If the teacher doesn't pick her she gets very disappointed but tries all the harder, but when she is picked she cannot stop talking and tells the teacher everything she knows, whether relevant to the topic or not. She does not like being stopped in mid-flow and reacts with confusion. Her interventions tend to cause some hilarity among her classmates as she speaks in a peculiar high pitched and very loud voice. The safest strategy for the teacher is not to invite a contribution from her.

Relationships with parents

Partnership with parents is a key ingredient in supporting children's learning and the ability to cope with the social and emotional passage between home and school. Parents' evenings were, for many however, the only source of contact and typically teachers had not met with the parents before taking the child into their class. Teachers were, in many instances, able to benefit from parental advice as special needs and could on occasions offer counsel on how to support learning and manage behaviour in the home environment. However, advising a parent on how to cope with Down's children, children on the Asperger's spectrum or with ADHD or complex learning needs, was an intimidating prospect for teachers who confessed to being out of their depth yet wanting to help parents often in distress and lacking in information or initiative where to turn for expert help. In areas with good strategic facilities, with collaborative working relationships, with special schools or with an accessible local authority, teachers could get support, but as we discovered, pressures on other agencies attempts at communication could be more frustrating than helpful. The commitment to keep children within the mainstream, seeking appropriate support, brought with it a huge investment of time and energy.

Contacts with parents were typically concerned with behavioural rather than learning-related issues and consultation with parents was often seen not as a means of decreasing workload and classroom problems but rather as an additional source of stress. Where teachers did have a closer relationship with parents this involved a lot of extra time, not only in face-to-face meetings but in telephoning, writing reports and liaising with psychological and social services. While such responsibilities often fell to a SENCO, a senior member of staff, or someone with a specific remit, typically parents wanted direct contact with the teacher.

The resilience needed to work constructively with parents proved to be highly dependent on the context in which those meetings took place. In schools where there were supportive parents and a critical mass of well-adjusted children the ability to cope with children who acted out their frustrations was very different from schools in highly disadvantaged areas where a large percentage, even a majority of pupils, had high levels of need. In schools, serving areas of multiple disadvantage teachers had to deal not only with frequent confrontation with children but sometimes with their parents too.

While many of the anecdotes of assault, alcoholism, drugs, firearms and gang warfare, are the stuff of lurid headlines, it was also a reality for teachers in some areas of cities and outer suburbs. The balance of intake was compounded by schools that were seen as dumping grounds, taking in pupils excluded by other schools, some of whom were keen to maintain their attainment profiles. This is termed the law of 'unnatural proportion' in which social, economic and housing policies 'ghettoise' parents and children, concentrating and compounding the effects of poverty and the associated health and welfare issues that go with it. For schools located in these communities, on the edge of the social and educational mainstream, 'inclusion' has to be understood within a context of socio-economic exclusion. These are places where 'special needs' and individual needs meet and may be hard to discern, and where the roots of 'extreme' behaviour are complex and multi-layered.

Issues of expertise and professional development

There is a significant lack of expertise and professional development in meeting a wide spectrum of needs. The importance of professional development, and lack of it, was consistently raised by teachers, heads and TAs as a critical issue if inclusion policies were to have any prospect of success. School staff were too often left to fall back on common sense or 'instinct'.

> There is very little specialist training. You do what you can instinctively but very often that isn't good enough. It's not good enough for the assistant because they feel inadequate and it's not good enough for the child. (TA, primary school)

A primary teacher talked about positive handling and the training they received which, she said, was totally inappropriate to most of situations they encountered. A training session with much theory and practising of moves with compliant adults was not transferable to the wildly out-of-control child, biting and kicking and causing a danger to himself and to staff. The spontaneity and volatility of these situations, sometimes with no other support available, did not, as staff said, usually follow textbook rules.

The lack of specialist expertise and professional development emerged as a constant strand in virtually every written or verbal comment from teachers and LSAs. We are reminded of a policy change under the Thatcher government when Kenneth Baker as Secretary of State for Education instructed University Education Departments to close down courses for graduates specifically trained to support children with learning difficulties on the grounds that every would-be teacher had to train in one of the core or foundation subjects in the new National Curriculum. Ministry officials argued that it was more appropriate to gain expertise in aspects of teaching children with special needs after a suitable induction period of teaching 'normal classes' by means of an in-service diploma or Masters' qualification. However, while the proportion of children requiring specialised support has increased, the specialist knowledge and qualifications have not kept pace.

Is inclusion working?

Amidst the myriad problems cited by teachers there were many positives. Those cited by teachers were:

- Social benefits to children and young people from being more accepted by their peers and by adults;
- Social benefits to children and young people who come to a better under-standing and acceptance of people with special needs;
- A broader professional awareness of diversity of needs and learning difficul-ties;
- Enhancement of teachers' and LSAs' repertoire of skills in dealing with a diversity of special needs;
- Parental satisfaction from feeling their children are being educated within the community alongside their neighbours' children.

Seeing things through a positive lens, there was evidence that having to accommodate a range of special needs had helped teachers to be more perceptive, more flexible, accommodating and ultimately more learner-centred.

> It does make you a better teacher because it raises your patience threshold. It forces you to try new strategies, new techniques and to be the best teacher you can be to keep that child with you. (Reception teacher)

Such 'value-added', as one member of staff put it, was often bought at a heavy price, however. In virtually all cases the benefits enumerated above required some qualification. Learning to cope with diversity was a professional plus for teachers **but** only if there was a culture and support to allow teachers to realise the benefits. There were clearly social benefits for many pupils **but** only where conditions were right and where special needs did not create resistance and resentment. Parental satisfaction was rewarding too **but** only where special needs were such that they could be met adequately within the mainstream and teachers' efforts were appreciated. For these benefits to be realised it relied on a quality of leadership, goodwill among teachers and a shared cultural belief that inclusion could, within reasonable bounds, be a force for good.

Even in the most positive of schools, however, questions remained as to the viability of policy which had not given adequate thought to the impact on teachers' work and job satisfaction. While the positives refer primarily to social and learning benefits owed to the efforts and goodwill of teachers and school leaders, the concerns all point to systemic issues which work at cross grain to the essential purpose of inclusion.

 Questions for discussion

Which of the following resonate with your own experience?

- Lack of entitlement to learn and develop emotionally and intellectually for children with special needs;
- Restriction of entitlement for learning for children who appeared to be coping well and were less demanding;
- Lack of acknowledgement of the needs of children without 'Special Needs' in that a disproportionate amount of time is given to a few;
- Feeling of inadequacy among teachers who recognised their lack of specialist expertise;
- Pressure on school staff due to inadequate resourcing by government and local authorities;
- 'Successful' schools attracting parents of SEN children and reaching a critical mass;
- Inadequate and inappropriate professional development;
- Heightened tensions between the inclusion and testing agendas;
- Increased workload among teachers, LSAs and senior leaders.

Workload Agreements and the Rise of the Teaching Assistant

In the early years of the new Millennium, Government Ministers conceded that the pressure on teachers had become intolerable and that measures needed to be taken to ease up on government demands on the one hand, and relieve teachers of some of the more routine and irksome administrative tasks on the other. The ensuing workload agreement sets the context for this chapter which charts the rise in prominence of teaching assistants.

Restructuring the workforce

The realisation that all was not well in schools was brought home to government ministers in the form of a presentation by teachers and head teachers to the Government Task Force on Standards which included at that time (2000) four highly influential Labour ministers, David Blunkett, Estelle Morris, Jackie Smith and Charles Clark. PricewaterhouseCoopers (PwC), commissioned to investigate the nature and extent of the issue, reported in 2001.

Following the publication of the PwC report (2001), the Labour government began negotiations with the teacher unions and Local Authority employers with the aim of restructuring the teaching workforce. The process which is known as *remodelling* aimed, according to Stevenson (2007:225), at 'reconfiguring teachers' work and remuneration to create a new division of labour within the pedagogical process, allowing teachers to focus their efforts on the core tasks of teaching and learning. Central to this reconfiguration was the increased use of non-qualified staff to work alongside teachers in what were described as 'various supporting roles'. Other associated reforms, such as the increased use of information and communications technology (ICT) would, it was argued, also support teaching and reduce the administrative burden (Selwood and Pilkington, 2005).

The Department for Education and Skills published the National Agreement in January 2003 (DfES, 2003b). This envisaged a three-stage remodelling process. In the first stage (September 2003) teachers were to be relieved of some 24 routine clerical tasks, such as collecting money, bulk photocopying, chasing absences, looking after ICT equipment and various duties associated with examining and testing such as data processing. Reasonable allowance was also to be made for management and leadership responsibilities (Butt and Gunter, 2005). The next phase (September 2004) envisaged schools tackling the 'cover problem' so that non-contact time would be protected, with a ceiling of 38 hours in any one year. The final stage (September 2005) sought to guarantee 10 per cent 'professional non-contact time' for planning, preparation and assessment tasks (PPA time). For primary school staff, in particular, this latter reform had far reaching implications in redeployment and resourcing, since up to now teachers had been timetabled to work every teaching session.

There have been a number of evaluations designed to monitor the success of the agreement. The Transforming the School Workforce Pathfinder Projects was set up as a pilot in 2002 while negotiations for the National Agreement were still ongoing. Extra resources were provided to employ additional support staff in the 32 primary and secondary schools and to train teachers in the use of more sophisticated forms of ICT. In the primary school workloads were reduced by an average of 3.5 hours and teachers appeared to have a more positive view about their roles despite lingering uncertainties as to tasks that could be left to teaching assistants (Thomas *et al.*, 2004). Bach *et al.* (2006:1) were also sceptical, but conceded that the use of classroom-based TAs was pivotal to attempts to reform the workforce. Particular concern was expressed however, over the role of HLTAs who, under the redrafted regulations, were now able to undertake a range of teaching duties, including whole class teaching in specified circumstances (HMSO, 2003). In 2007, Frean reported that were now 150,000 TAs: two for every three qualified teachers.

In 2006, the Teachers Review Body (Office of Manpower and Economics, 2006) reported that over the period 2000–2005 primary teachers' workloads had dropped by just under two hours (from 52.8 to 50.9), the significant change coming in 2004 when PPA time was introduced. For primary head teachers there was a reported decrease in workload from 58.9 hours per week in 2002 to 53.5 hours in 2006. The amount of teaching by primary heads fell from six to four hours.

Evidence of success? Or learning on the cheap?

As our visits to schools and conversations with teachers and TAs reveal, the Workforce Agreement has had some tangible benefits. PPA time has been highly welcomed in some schools. In a primary school in the north-east of England, for example, teachers professed to a sea change in the culture of the school and the morale of staff. Once a week every teacher has PPA time for one half-day so that at 12 p.m. they could, if they wished, leave school and go home. While they still do work at home in the evenings it was said that this is now undertaken 'without resentment'. Other teachers continued to stay and work in the staffroom as it gave them access to resources and web surfing, although also subject to interruption and ad hoc demands.

This liberation of teachers has, nonetheless, been bought at a price. In part it has created extra pressures for senior managers but more significantly has extended the role of unqualified staff, many of whom are the first to admit to their lack of requisite expertise and the anxiety that a teaching job involves.

> I am just thrown in to do a lesson and when it's over I often say to myself 'God, I'm rubbish' and feel totally inadequate stepping into someone else's shoes like that. Three days training didn't quite do it for me. (HLTA, 10 years' experience)

The ad hoc use of TAs is, however increasingly uncommon as 'cover' has now been built into structures and planning. In secondary schools buying in expensive specialist cover at £180 a day is being replaced by cover managers and cover teams, often comprised of TAs and HLTAs. In some cases, cover supervisors are given lesson plans to follow while in others pupils are left with set work so that, as some TAs described it, it was more a case of 'baby sitting'. There were also instances in secondary schools of cover supervisors teaching a class over an extended period of weeks.

TAs and cover supervisors (often one and the same thing) may receive in-school development courses on behaviour management but this is time consuming and a further source of pressure on teaching staff, as some TAs by their own admission were unsuited to the role, resulting in a high rate of turnover. 'They get demoralised and leave', said one member of staff, lamenting a constant cycle of training, retraining and support for new appointees. As a matter of necessity cover supervisors are obliged to operate without adequate training or support, falling back on common sense and family experience. As one TA put it 'I've drawn on my experience as a mum.'

The extent to which TAs 'teach' or actively support individual and group learning varies considerably from school to school but there are many instances where a TA is involved most of the time in a teaching role of one kind or another, generally with children of lower ability or children with special needs. 'I spend. I should say, 95% of my time working with lower ability children'. (TA, 13 years' experience)

Often the combination of work is divided between support for an individual child and work with a lower ability group.

> My primary role is working with a child who has a statement for 15 hours. A lot of the lessons she doesn't need one to one support so I work with the

gold group which is the lower ability group. When any writing is involved I tend to work with that group of children. I also do the reading schemes for those children which is reading and comprehension questions. (TA, 7 years' experience)

While teachers would like to draw on TAs for the range of support promised they often find that the TA has been fully occupied with a child with complex needs, 'glued so tightly', as one teacher put it, that she was unavailable to teaching staff.

At the beginning of the year we didn't have enough TA hours at all. I've got a full time TA in my class because I have a very autistic child so she is one to one. She is glued to his side – so that in a way takes out the TA time that I could have had from her – doing little jobs for me. (Key Stage 1 teacher)

A Key Stage 2 colleague in the same school echoed the complaint, claiming that essentially nothing has changed – 'I spend a lot of time at the photocopier still but if I don't do it, who does?' The irony is that TAs brought in to relieve teachers of the more routine administrative task now enjoy a curious role reversal, with teachers in some cases doing their own paperwork and photocopying to free up TAs to work with children.

My TA is not a general. She doesn't do any photocopying or put displays up for me at all. She works with groups of children. Which makes my workload heavy because then I do my own photocopying. I'm in at 7.30 every morning. (Key Stage 1 teacher)

Weighing the balance between time 'off' and time with the class, some teachers felt that the loss of quality teaching was too high.

Sometimes it would be easier to teach rather than have PPA. (Key Stage 2 teacher, 28 years' experience)

PPA time benefits me but it doesn't benefit the children. When there are specialists like the Italian teacher or the drumming lesson, that's OK but we leave 'easy' work for children to do when TAs are taking the class. (Key Stage 2 teacher, 8 years' experience)

We're a profession now

'We're profession now, not second class citizens', said one TA, speaking in the context of a working week taken up primarily with small group, whole class and one-to-one teaching. Yet, at the same time these support staff are badly paid, largely untrained, insecure in their job tenure and often treated dismissively despite the workload and pressures they now share with their teaching colleagues.

Teachers' workload has been eased but ours has shot up. We now come in earlier and work later and our conditions of employment have got much worse.

> Although we take work home and also work on a lot of evenings, we are now being paid only for days worked and not for holidays. (HLTA, 10 years' experience)

Another HLTA describes her job as 'slave labour' encompassing, among the 24 tasks on her schedule, medication, behaviour review, responding to queries from teachers, dealing with parental complaints, organising parent evenings, sorting out food, managing resources, fund raising, setting up classrooms, organising, managing and supervising and assessing TAs as well as class cover. She expresses surprise at the apparent willingness of TAs to continue with their high level of commitment in the face of 'miserable' and 'denigrating' pay.

> I know one thing that really annoys TAs about work here is the extra we are paid for PPA time is about 20p or something. I haven't claimed a single hours' worth of PPA time since September – it's just not worth it. (TA, 7 years' experience)

This is compounded by insecurity of the TAs position in the school, dependent on funding often through the numbers of children with statements. Management is faced with having to juggle the numbers of TAs they are able to have with the money available. Many have had their hours reduced due to lack of funding. As a result: 'Some of them who lost hours feel very, very bitter.' (TA, 5 years' experience)

The 24 tasks

Collecting money

Chasing absences – teachers will need to inform the relevant member of staff when students are absent from their class or from school.

Bulk photocopying

Copy typing

Producing standard letters – teachers may be required to contribute as appropriate in formulating the content of standard letters.

Producing class lists – teachers may be required to be involved as appropriate in allocating students to a particular class.

Record keeping and filing – teachers may be required to contribute to the content of records.

Continued

Continued

Classroom display – teachers will make professional decisions in determining what material is displayed in and around their classroom.

Analysing attendance figures – it is for teachers to make use of the outcome of analysis.

Processing exam results – teachers will need to use the analysis of exam results.

Collating pupil reports.

Administering work experience – teachers may be required to support pupils on work experience (including through advice and visits).

Administering examinations – teachers have a professional responsibility for identifying appropriate examinations for their pupils.

Administering teacher cover.

ICT trouble shooting and minor repairs.

Commissioning new ICT equipment.

Ordering supplies and equipment – teachers may be involved in identifying needs.

Stocktaking.

Cataloguing, preparing, issuing and maintaining equipment and materials.

Minuting meetings – teachers may be required to communicate action points from meetings.

Co-ordinating and submitting bids – teachers may be required to make a professional input into the content of bids.

Seeking and giving personnel advice.

Managing pupil data – teachers will need to make use of the analysis of pupil data.

Inputting pupil data – teachers will need to make the initial entry of pupil data into school management systems.

There were also comments in some schools about a hierarchy of status among HTLAs, TAs, Classroom Assistants and unhappiness in relation to perceived differences in the amount and intensity of work. For example, some TAs have to work with small groups of children most of the day while others spend time photocopying, organising resources and listening to children reading. Some of this disparity in the nature and range of work was ascribed to teacher-TA relationships. While some spoke of excellent and supportive relationships, others felt that they were treated dismissively and like 'dogsbodies'. 'Sometimes I feel like a 'dogsbody' and have to do whatever is needed at a given time.' (TA working in Key Stage 2)

While some schools had created a career path for TAs, including appointment as SENCOs, with the possibility of attaining advanced level status in pastoral care, for many the combination of low pay, greater responsibility, high workloads and lack of advancement prospects added up to a lowering of morale and a search for more satisfying employment.

A remodelled secondary school

As an example we provide a case study of one particular secondary school. The head, who has been in this school seven years, believes that Workforce Remodelling has not improved work-life balance (he works a 70-hour week) but has brought a new focus through restructuring of roles. The head has re-organised progressively from the top down, reshaping governors' meetings by creating small working sub-committees with specific remits. 'Bringing right people on board' included the appointment of a highly efficient Business Manager with 'a flexible and creative approach to staff deployment.' Together with the senior leadership team they have developed a new cadre of 'rapid response' people who could be trusted to do their jobs with support and career path development. The ratio is now 70 teaching staff to 85 non-teaching staff, the latter with highly differentiated roles including Technicians, TAs, HLTAs, Learning Mentors, Assistant Learning Mentors, Progress Managers, Standards Managers and Learning Managers.

There are now no Heads of Year but Key Stage Teachers and Curriculum Leaders, supported by Standards Managers and Progress Managers, described as 'front-end preventative rather than back-end reactive'. Progress managers are non-teaching staff who have progressed through the Learning Mentor route, previously volunteer parents or TAs or lunchtime supervisors, for example. They support teaching staff through monitoring of student performance, referring students at risk to the Key Stage Leader, organising work experience, making contact with parents and referring troublesome students to her counterpart, the Standards Manager. The Standards Manager takes on the pastoral aspect of what was once the Head of Department's role, monitoring behaviour, managing inclusion, advising and issuing sanctions 'like a parent' and reporting to the Assistant Head responsible for pastoral care, him/herself having progressed through the Learning Mentor, Progress Manager career route. These managers oversee achievement, and behaviour, monitoring through a traffic lights system, every child in the school with, as a reference point, appropriate colour coding so that targets and support can be personalised.

There are five Learning Managers who work as a team to provide cover. These are staff who have progressed from roles as TAs or other 'non-qualified' staff (although one has a degree in politics), and in some cases graduates sampling teaching for two years before doing their PGCE. They work as a team, covering classes where they feel most able to teach or supervise the curricular subject. In cases where there is advance knowledge of absence, teachers leave them a lesson plan. For unplanned absences they rely on their experience and knowledge of the pupils to teach the class. They argue that their relationship with pupils and their knowledge of the school, developed over time, puts them in a stronger position than cover teachers brought in for a day or two. They may cover up to 20 lessons a week and their day is similar to teachers, starting at around 7.45 a.m. with 'trouble shooting' and ending around 5 p.m. but also extending to two nights week to homework clubs and also to ad hoc meetings with parents. 'Teachers tell us they wouldn't do our job for the world' says one Learning Manager, pointing to a high level of turnover in what is a demanding and undersalaried job for which there is no holiday pay.

Promise unfulfilled

Reviewing each of the tenets of the Agreement the evidence is at best equivocal:

- Teachers cannot routinely be required to undertake administrative and clerical tasks – teacher time is more exclusively devoted to high-quality professional teaching tasks.

As we have seen, teachers do undertake administrative tasks for a variety of reasons – because TAs are totally preoccupied with ('glued to') a single child, or are working with a specific group of children, or are too busy elsewhere or sometimes simply unavailable. Teachers still engage in a range of administrative tasks because some choose to do things which are seen as integral to their teaching (putting up pupils' work on the wall, for example) and because delegation often proves more time consuming than doing it yourself. In addition, the nature of highly pressurised, complex and wholly unpredictable school life means that teachers have to think, plan on their feet and take whatever course of action a situation demands.

- A work-life balance clause which entitles teachers to achieve a reasonable balance between the time required to discharge their professional duties and the time required to pursue their personal interests outside work.

There is some evidence that PPA in particular has contributed to a better work-life balance but there is evidence elsewhere that little has changed, particularly in secondary schools and particularly where PPA time is swallowed up by increasing pressures of disruptive behaviour and ill-conceived inclusion policies.

Where teachers are happier it appears to be explained by the ability of head-teachers and senior leaders to work creatively to create space for teachers, both by taking on more work themselves and/or deploying TAs to cover teachers' absences.

- Leadership and management time for all teachers at a school with leadership and management responsibilities – giving them a reasonable allocation of time within school sessions to support the discharge of their responsibilities.
- Dedicated headship time specifically for head teachers, particularly those with a teaching commitment of over 50 per cent, giving head teachers time to lead, as well as manage, their schools.

There is scant evidence from our studies that head teachers and others in management positions have benefited. Indeed they appear to be under greater pressure than before, in part to arrange for teachers to have more professional development time, in part to manage TA arrangements and in large part to attend to mounting demands on headship from policy initiatives on the one hand, and from community and parental pressures on the other.

- A guaranteed minimum of 10 per cent of time within the timetabled teaching day for planning, preparation and assessment (PPA) – to relieve some of the existing workload pressures on teachers and to support high-quality teaching. This is guaranteed time that must not be used for any other activity, including cover for absent colleagues.

Much depends on how that 10 per cent is organised. Where schools can provide a half-day block it can be dedicated time for planning and preparation and if there is a suitable space, in some cases at home, that time may be used productively. The occasional 'period' or hour off in the day does not always achieve the objective, however, as the realities of school life intrude. There is not always the dedicated space and teachers find themselves interrupted and having to attend to other things and, as we have seen in the secondary context (Chapter 5), protected time is more a myth than a reality.

A case for a more differentiated profession?

Schools and classrooms are no longer the sole preserve of teachers. The world is changing. The financing of schools is changing. Demands on teachers have increased beyond their capacity to meet them. The very nature of schools for the future is open to question and the traditional conception of a teacher and his or her own class may no longer be a tenable model in the future. The argument for a more differentiated profession is a compelling one, allowing people with differing responsibilities to play to their strengths, affirming the higher-level skills of teachers and heads and providing them with the space to develop professionally. Schools have, for a long time, enjoyed a whole range of staff with distinctive job remits and responsibilities – office staff, caretakers, cleaners, lunchtime supervisors, bursars and teaching assistants together with volunteer parents and often others in voluntary roles supporting and advancing the work of the school. However as we have seen from the proliferation of roles, not only is 'the core task' reconfigured in ways that constrain and diminish the nature of pedagogy but much of that core task is now being assumed by unqualified staff.

As Table 8.1 shows (taken from the most recent school census) there is an almost exponential increase in support staff. On closer inspection it may be inferred that the largest increases are in the most poorly paid sectors – TAs, clerical staff other than secretaries, part-time teaching staff and overseas teachers without teaching qualifications. Table 8.2 juxtaposes this with numbers of qualified full-time and part-time teachers in primary and secondary schools.

Table 8.1 Support staff in the maintained sector in England by type of contract (January of each year, percentages). DfES, 2005, Annual Census, London: Department for Education and Schools

Categories of support staff	1997	1998	1999	2000	2001	2002	2003	2004	2005
Teaching assistants	35.5	38.8	39.3	45.3	55.6	57.3	73.2	84.1	96.8
SEN support staff	24.5	26.0	29.5	32.4	37.7	46.7	46.8	46.9	48.1
Minority ethnic support staff	1.2	1.5	1.5	2.1	2.5	2.5	2.5	2.5	2.5
Secretaries	27.6	28.5	29.1	30.2	30.6	25.6	24.7	28.6	28.3
Bursars	4.1	4.2	4.4	4.7	5.0	4.9	5.1	5.7	6.3
Other clerical staff	7.5	7.3	7.7	8.3	10.7	19.3	20.8	20.2	24.0
Medical staff	1.2	1.2	1.2	1.2	1.2	1.8	1.7	1.9	1.9
3.4	3.4	3.4	3.1	3.3	3.2	3.2	0.4	1.7	2.9
Other (e.g. librarians, technicians)	18.7	19.7	22.1	23.1	27.4	39.3	32.3	32.0	34.0

Table 8.2 Teachers in the maintained sector in England by type of contract (January of each year, thousands). DfES, 2005, Annual Census, London: Department for Education and Schools

	1997	1998	1999	2000	2001	2002	2003	2004	2005
Primary and nursery									
Qualified regular teachers	190.7	189.0	189.9	191.6	192.6	193.1	191.9	190.4	190.1
Full-time	175.8	173.9	173.9	174.7	174.6	173.9	171.5	168.7	167.1
Part-time	14.8	15.0	15.9	16.8	17.9	19.1	20.3	21.8	23.0
Overseas teachers without QTS	0.8	0.9	1.0	1.2	1.8	2.9	3.9	3.9	4.1
Secondary									
Qualified regular teachers	187.7	187.7	187.7	191.1	193.8	196.6	197.9	200.6	203.8
Full-time	174.2	173.8	175.6	176.5	179.1	181.2	182.2	183.9	186.2
Part-time	13.4	13.8	14.1	14.5	14.6	15.3	15.7	16.7	17.5
Overseas teachers without QTS	1.5	1.6	1.9	1.8	2.3	4.7	6.4	6.9	7.2

The balance of staffing in schools is clearly undergoing a seismic change. The Government argument is that this is not only inevitable but highly desirable and that schools are most likely to improve through effective deployment of these various players, further developing and enhancing individual and joint capacity. In 2006 the DfES, celebrating the implementation of the 'historic' Agreement reported as follows:

> Schools which have successfully implemented workforce remodelling have recognised that the contractual changes for teachers and headteachers and the principles at the heart of the Agreement are designed to raise standards by enabling teachers and headteachers to focus on their core roles of teaching and of leading teaching and learning. An important and integral part of school improvement is enhanced roles for support staff who are qualified professionals in their own right, playing an important role in the education team. (Raising Standards and Tackling Workload Implementing the National Agreement, Note 16, DfES, 16 June 2006)

While our study is a limited one, we do not believe it unrepresentative because the issues we raise have a systemic basis in government ideology and the 'delivery' of public services. Education, like other services is 'delivered' and in the interest of making this a more cost-effective process workforce remodelling has been at the heart of government efforts to reform public services. Smith (2005) puts it this way:

> The basic concern is, on the one hand, to make those working in public services more disposed to the implementation of government policies (rather than what might they might discern as being right for the individual, group and community). On the other hand, there is a desire to contain costs. The result has been an attempt to remove areas of professional discretion (through the implementation of procedures, common assessment frameworks and the like); to shift responsibility for the 'delivery' of key elements of education to those less expensive and less skilled practitioners (the use of the word 'delivery' here immediately transforms education from a process to a product); and to encourage flexible working patterns.

The division of labour, it has been argued (for example, Butt and Gunter, 2005; Stevenson, 2007), serves to create a divorce between those who plan and those who execute, between teaching and pastoral care. Behind the design of a highly structured business-like delivery system lies a grand narrative, the so-called Third Way and the 'new professionalism'. This international current of ideas envisages a highly differentiated public service, more efficient in ensuring outcomes and meeting targets. Intrinsic to it is the creation of a multi-tier labour market with a large, and widening, salary gap between those who manage from the top, those who manage from the middle, those who teach (including Advanced Skills teachers and excellent teachers) and the supporting cast who play their own role in labour substitution.

The price for liberating teachers from routine tasks has, however, been to tie them more closely to expedient measures of performance, linking pay more explicitly to performance, a 'technical delivery of subject content and the achievement of pre-specified learning outcomes' (Stevenson, 2007:236). The 'freeing up of teachers' has to be seen within a prescriptive and pressurised environment, where teachers are willing to apply themselves more assiduously to curricula, assessment and formulaic lessons in return for their new partnership status. 'Teachers now expect lessons to be sourced from elsewhere. They don't know how to plan a lesson,' charges Stevenson (2007:236), citing evidence of a growing trend for teachers to download lesson plans from the DCSF website. While this is a generalisation of a high order and clearly not applicable everywhere, it does reflect an underlying concern about a 'centralised pedagogy' and 'diminishes the space in which teachers can, or need to, exercise professional judgement' (p. 235).

While the idea of the Social Partnership was widely welcomed there were some dissenting voices. The Pricewaterhousecoopers Workload Study signalled potential dangers in the use of unqualified staff. A Warwick University study published findings in 2002 reported that 85 per cent of teachers welcomed additional administrative support but 79 per cent were against the prospect of teaching assistants covering for teacher absences.

In the Australian context, Sachs (2003), has argued that governments gain their legitimacy through the promulgation of policies and the allocation of funds associated with those policies. The 'modern professional' works efficiently to meet the standardised criteria and outcomes for student attainment in line with the school's formal accountability procedures. Her comments appear to reflect closely the situation in England as characterised by numerous commentators and by our own findings in successive studies between 2002 and 2007.

Teachers' bargaining position and voice have been progressively diminished, and most worryingly, we discern through teachers' accounts a widespread resignation to one's professional lot, as one teacher put it:

> Once you have expended all your energy in increasingly confrontative behaviour, dealing with irate parents, making up work for TAs, supervising them, filling out the hundredth form what energy is there left to fight the government? You might just begin to believe there is a conspiracy of silence afoot. But I couldn't possibly say that.

 Questions for discussion

On balance has workforce remodelling been a good or bad thing? What do you see as the pros and cons?

What, in your view, are appropriate roles for non-teaching staff? To what extent do teaching qualifications matter?

Counting the hours is of much less importance if the nature of the work is satisfying. Do you agree?

It's the Same the Whole World Over: What Happens in Other Countries?

This chapter examines research on teachers' working lives in four other countries (Canada, Hong Kong, Australia and New Zealand) all with certain similarities to UK schooling, practices subsumed from the period when these countries had formal links with the crown. The fact that workloads are increasing despite the different forms of governance (central vs federal), schooling (primary vs secondary) and classroom organisation (mixed ability vs streams and bands) suggests that there may be underlying common features beyond the bureaucratic and administrative procedures that are seen as the prime cause of teachers' dissatisfaction.

The Canadian experience

Canada is not only a country of ten provinces (and three territories) but is also a country with 13 different educational systems. While there is a Federal Ministry, major decisions about school provision, curriculum and the teaching force are taken at the provincial level with the day-to-day running of schools devolved to school districts. These are in some respects analogous to local authorities in the UK but alongside large city school districts are very small school districts serving no more than a cluster of local schools but with a stronger directive influence on school decision-making than in English LAs, as devolved management has not gone as far as it has in England.

Canada bears many similarities to Australia in its geographical diversity, with its significant Aboriginal (or 'first nation') population, its patterns of elementary/primary schools and comprehensive high schools, although differing in respect of public/private provision, with only 8 per cent of children in private schools in Canada compared with more than a third in Australia. What is common to both, however, and to the other countries discussed here, are increasing difficulties in recruitment and retention of staff, with workload and stress cited as key 'dissatisfiers'.

In 2001, PricewaterhouseCooper used the Canadian experience as a benchmark, basing their judgements mainly from Canadian reports where reforms in many of its provinces paralleled those in the UK and tended to provoke similar responses. They concluded that in relation to Canada, teacher hours in England and Wales appear to be relatively higher although the underling issues were very similar and of greater consequence than simple differences in number of hours worked.

Reports from different Canadian provinces reveal similar patterns and common underlying issues. For example, a British Columbia study (Naylor and Malcolmson, 2001; Naylor and Schaefer, 2003) reported excessive workload as the main cause of teacher stress. They identified the sheer volume of work, the wide range of workload duties, changing class composition and continuous disruptive incidents as the main contributors to stress, in some cases leading to a major breakdown in health. These authors concluded that:

- Far too great an emphasis had been placed on change and expectations, without any consideration of the manageability of such change for teachers.
- There was disillusionment with a profession that for many respondents is clearly a vocation, and not just a job. This stems from the fact that though they cared deeply about the students in our schools, they increasingly believed that nobody appears to care greatly about teachers.

A poll of public opinion sponsored by the Canadian Teachers Federation (CTF 2003) reported that:

- Sixty-nine per cent believed that the increased workload for high school teachers was very likely or somewhat likely to result in inconsistency of instruction for students;
- Sixty per cent believed this increased workload is just another example of the government moving too fast;
- Sixty-eight per cent believed that the increased workload has resulted in an increase in homework for teachers as they prepare for the extra class and evaluate the extra students; and
- Sixty-one per cent believed the teacher argument that the increased workload means less remedial help for students.

Other studies reach similar conclusions – Harvey and Spinney (2000) in Nova Scotia (NS), LeBlanc (2000) in New Brunswick (NB), Billivieu *et al.* (2002) in

Table 9.1 Time spent out of school on various activities in Canadian schools

Activity	PEI (hours)	NS (hours)	BC (hours)	NL (hours)
Preparation	7.10	7.50	7.60	9.25
Marking and report writing	7.80	9.20	11.50	6.30
Meetings	1.60	2.30	2.00	2.30
Supervision	2.75	2.90	n/a	3.85
Totals	19.25	21.90	21.10	21.70
Total weekly workload	52.00 (max)	52.50	53.10	52.32

Prince Edward Island (PEI) and Dibbon (2004) in Newfoundland and Labrador (NL) (see Table 9.1). In Nova Scotia teachers complained that the intensification of teaching resulted in insufficient time to prepare lessons adequately, and that special needs pupils, in particular, were neglected. In the New Brunswick survey the main concerns had to do with the size of classes and the proliferation of paperwork mainly involving marking and grading. Teachers from Prince Edward Island reported that, compared to five years earlier, workload had increased significantly, mainly due to an increase in discipline problems, more administrative tasks and meetings with parents. Dibbon's 2004 survey cited lack of planning time, large classes and problems of dealing with a wide range of ability in mixed age/ability classes, inappropriate assignments and targets associated with too many new programmes and curriculum initiatives. He reported an increase of between 5 and 6 hours compared to the overall weekly workload in the mid-nineties when it averaged 47 hours weekly.

The Canadian Teachers' Federation Workplace survey (CTF, 2003) concluded that 60 per cent of teachers found their jobs more stressful than two years previously, with increased workload as the major cause of stress and a primary reasons for leaving the profession. The 52-hour weeks (compared to 47 hours in the CTF 2001 survey) are slightly less than those of the PricewaterhouseCooper estimate of 54 hours for English teachers (PwC, 2001), but the disillusionment felt by Canadian colleagues seems to be less to do with number of hours worked than with the nature and range of what is expected of teachers and the changing social context of the classroom. This becomes a recurring theme as we move from country to country. The issues play out in surprisingly similar ways in Hong Kong.

The Hong Kong experience

The development of the Hong Kong education system is a remarkable success story. Starting from a low base at the end of the Second World War and, until recently, with an ever-increasing expanding population it has managed to provide universal education up to the age of 16 including kindergarten for most children up to the age of six. Since 1997, Hong Kong and its associated New Territories were returned to China and it now exists as a Special Autonomous Region (SAR) with complete control over its education system and with its own Curriculum Development Institute (CDI), similar to the Qualifications and Curriculum Authority (QCA) in England.

Despite the problems of providing mass education for a large population, Hong Kong pupils have performed extremely well in various international comparative studies, such as Third International Mathematics and Science Study (TIMSS) and the more percent OECD Programme for International Students Assessment (PISA). In mathematics, Hong Kong regularly occupy one of the top five places out of around 40 countries at both primary and lower secondary levels. Schools are large in comparison with those in the UK. For example, a typical primary school can have a seven form entry with classes of 35 pupils or more, starting at the age of six in P1 and going through to P6. Teachers generally teach their specialist subject across the entire age range, unlike the Canadian system which follows the UK pattern of having a class teacher who covers most lessons.

At the beginning of the millennium the Education Commission instituted a series of changes in the curriculum starting in the primary phase in 2001. Under the title, *Learning for Life – Learning through Life*, the reforms sought to reduce the impact of testing, encouraging greater curriculum integration and the use of a broader range of teaching methods. Thus in some ways Hong Kong represents reform which, despite its international successes under the present format, was attempting to liberalise its education system, in stark contrast to what was taking place in many western countries where there was greater pressure for conformity and increasing use of testing as an indicator of public account-ability. In Hong Kong, for example, secondary schools are told of the average performance of their primary intake but the scores of individual pupils are not disclosed.

Despite these reforms, however, there have been constant complaints about the pressures and stress from teachers, leading to the setting up of a committee of enquiry by the Education and Manpower Bureau (recently renamed as the Education Development Bureau) (EMB, 2006). Just fewer than 4,200 individuals responded to the questionnaire of which 475 belonged to senior management or were school principals. Teachers said that they worked for ten hours each day during term time and for around 4.6 hours on non-school days, totaling 59.2 hours per week. An as yet unpublished study for P1–P3 primary confirms that workloads are formidable. On average, the working week for teachers was 63.5 hours comprised of:

- 16 hours a week teaching (27.3 periods, typically of 35 minutes duration);
- 14 hours planning lessons and marking pupils work;
- 19 hours on administrative matters (3 hours) lesson preparation (3 hours) and further marking (6.5 hours);
- 14½ hours at weekends in planning, marking work and dealing with admin-istrative issues.

The main difference between Hong Kong and English primary teachers is to be found in the amount of marking undertaken by the Hong Kong practitioners. English teachers spend 4.5 hours each week in marking pupils' work compared to the 14.5 hours spent by their Hong Kong counterparts. This difference alone can be seen to account for the disparity in workloads between the two primary school systems. Another interesting feature concerns the effect of class size (Galton, 2007). In almost every instance it was claimed by teachers that reducing class size was one of the most effective ways of reducing workload but teachers in classes of between 20 and 25 pupils have, in fact, marginally higher workloads than the reported EMB (2006) figure for both primary and secondary sectors. Teachers in the small class study said that although fewer pupils meant less marking, small classes involved more preparation time because additional resources were needed to cover greater use of co-operative groups and for dealing more effectively with the range of pupil abilities within the class.

The large-scale EMB survey in 2006 also constructed a *stress index*. Beginning teachers (1–2 years' experience) had the highest levels of stress, largely caused by increased emotion and anxiety over student-teacher relationships, mainly to do with discipline. Teachers with 5–9 years' experience were mostly concerned by 'professional distress' (the loss of professional autonomy) and time management. Older teachers (20 years' plus experience) seemed to have accepted the loss of professional autonomy and had fewest concerns about teacher-student relationships or time management.

The study also examined the impact of external factors such as curriculum innovation, expectations of external stakeholders such as parents, the impact of testing, school management and pupil diversity in terms of ability, attitudes and motivation. For beginning teachers the impact of these factors on stress levels was slight. For those with 5–9 years' experience school management factors (poor communication channels) and dealing with external stakeholders caused the greatest problems. For the most experienced teachers it was test-related factors, particularly the introduction of language proficiency tests for teachers in English and Putonghua (Mandarin) which gave rise to increased anxiety. Interestingly, there was no discernable pattern between the hours worked and the stress level.

The introduction of school self evaluation (SSE) and external school review (ESR, 2002) in both primary and secondary sectors has been closely monitored and evaluated over a four-year period (MacBeath and Clark, 2005). Data from over 70,000 teachers revealed that workload was 'the headline issue' and provoked by far the greatest number of write-in comments on questionnaires. The Impact Report to the Education Bureau cited the nature of complaints as primarily concerned with serial innovation, distracting teachers from their main classroom focus 'with documentation seen by many as too much, too complex, too detailed and too onerous' (MacBeath, 2007:32).

Coping with stress rarely results in teachers seeking outside help. Many teachers appeared to feel that there was a stigma attached to those who seek professional counseling help. For the most part teachers tended to adopt a 'make the best of it' attitude by emphasising the positives and working even harder or give up on the problem and resign themselves to the consequences. In the latter situation, as might be expected, stress levels were likely to increase.

Both the report of the committee of enquiry into workload (EMB, 2006) and the Impact report (MacBeath, 2007) make several observations which are germane to the situation in England, in particular, that mutual trust between policy makers and classroom practitioners is essential if the innovations are to proceed smoothly. As with Key Stage Strategies in England, Hong Kong teachers approve in principle of curriculum changes and the purposes of school self evaluation but are often unhappy at the way in which they have been implemented, feeling that too little faith has been placed on the teachers' own professional judgment. Allied to factors which threaten future employment (often referred to as 'filling the rice bowl'), declining birth rates, coupled with rising expectations within the community, had made their own contribution to increasing levels of stress, decreasing morale and job satisfaction, emanating in decreasing productivity and, in some cases, serious health problems. In listening to teachers' accounts we were reminded of Martin's book *The Sickening Mind* (1997) which found significant correlations between chronic illnesses such as heart conditions and cancer and the *perception* that one was no longer in control of one's own professional life and decision-making.

The New Zealand and Australian experience

Of all the countries discussed in this chapter New Zealand comes closest to the English system. It has a strong centrally directed curriculum, places emphasis on class teachers rather than specialists at primary level and has a national system of inspection (albeit with a lighter touch than Ofsted). In contrast, Australian education is strongly controlled by the various state administrations who resist central government's attempts to 'interfere' in the curriculum. National initiatives can only come about if the central authority can persuade states (usually by offering substantial financial resources) to co-operate.

In the case of New Zealand we are able to derive a national profile while in the Australian example we focus on what is happening in a particular state, Tasmania. Both examples have remote areas with isolated small rural schools where teachers are reluctant to work because of the lack of social and cultural amenities. Consequently, in Tasmania, it is the requirement of the teacher's contract that they must serve a proportion of the career in a rural establishment, unless there are exceptional circumstances that justify continued employment in an urban conurbation.

Workload issues have been a feature of the debate between the New Zealand Teacher Associations and the central government. As early as 1995 a survey carried out by the Post Primary Teachers Association (Ingvarson *et al.*, 2005) found that class teachers were working an average of 47.35 hours per week compared to 59.78 for middle managers. Only one-third of these hours were spent on classroom teaching. At the time, teachers perceived this workload as demanding, particularly the increase in administrative duties. Sixty per cent of 498 respondents said they would leave teaching if an opportunity arose.

The issue continued to be a source of disagreement between the Teacher Association and the Ministry of Education with several attempts by the latter to commission studies of 'best practice' until in 2004, during the re-negotiation of the secondary teachers' remuneration/workload 'Collective Agreement' it was decided to commission fresh research, carried out by the Australian Council of Educational Research (ACER).

The study by Ingvarson *et al.* (2005) involving a survey of 1,150 classroom teachers and 936 senior and middle managers found that classroom teachers worked an average of 47.1 hours weekly, middle managers 52.6 hours and senior managers 59.2 hours, with large degree of variation in each case. Table 9.2 shows the breakdown of these figures in terms of what were classified as *formally scheduled activities, professional activities* and *clerical activities*.

While the Ingvarson report does not explain some of the discrepancies in the table, the study goes on to elaborate on the nature of various activities. Formally scheduled activities included timetabled teaching time, participating in assemblies, cover, playground duty, meetings and supervision of students outside lessons (clubs, sport, school trips, etc.). Professional activities consisted of performance review, lesson planning, marking (including internal moderation and analysing student performance data) and professional development, dealing with student behaviour and other pastoral issues and communicating formally with parents.

Middle managers seemed to be most critical of their situation and the work-life balance. While some 71 per cent of teachers felt the workload affected the quality of their teaching and 66 per cent said they were unable to find the time to give professional help to colleagues, a slight majority (52 per cent) said that the work was manageable. New teachers with less than three years' experience appeared to be less concerned. Among middle managers, 47 per cent said that

Table 9.2 Breakdown of New Zealand secondary teachers' workloads by level of responsibility

Activity	S-manager (hours)	M-manager (hours)	Teacher (hours)
Formal scheduled activities	20.1	24.2	23.9
Professional activities	21.0	17.0	15.4
Clerical activities	10.8	8.6	7.7
Totals	51.9	49.8	47.0

work was seriously affecting their health and 27 per cent were thinking of leaving teaching to look for less stressful employment. These findings seemed unaffected by school size, school type, catchment area (in terms of social economic status), gender or ethnicity.

In a similar manner to the Hong Kong study, participants were asked to indicate what aspects of their work induced the greatest stress. The major factors contributing to stress appeared to be accountability reviews, and the manner of implementing change within the school. Moderate positive correlations were obtained between stress and relationships with parents, new government initiatives, class size and collating assessment data. As with the teachers in Hong Kong, stress levels were also found to be unrelated to the number of hours worked by teachers.

The Tasmanian study (Gardner and Williamson, 2004) employed a survey and asked teachers to keep diaries for one whole week. Primary teachers were working, on average 48.7 hours weekly and secondary teachers 52 hours (Table 9.3).

When asked to cite the major problems, both primary and secondary teachers listed intensification of teaching (especially the feeling of insufficient time to perform any of one's duties, particularly those in the classroom, in a satisfying manner), current policies of the Education Department, lack of resources and problem pupils.

Associated with this sense of intensification was the feeling of not being trusted to do a good job. This seems a constant theme in all the countries listed in this chapter and can be illustrated by a quotation from a Tasmanian primary teacher:

> There is a constant bombardment with pedagogy and ELF documents. 'You should be doing this', implying that what you have done before wasn't right. Staff morale is low. What's it all for? I've had experience of putting in time

Table 9.3 Comparison of workloads of Tasmanian teachers (primary vs secondary)

Activity	Primary (hours)	Secondary (hours)
Teaching	16.9	16.2
Planning/assessment	12.4	16.3
Administration	3.7	4.5
Professional learning	3.1	1.4
Supervision	2.4	1.4
Meetings	2.4	3.6
Discussions with colleagues	2.1	1.1
Discussions with parents	1.1	1.5
Extra curricular activities (clubs)	3.0	5.6
Other (e.g. mentoring trainees)	1.6	0.4
	48.7	52.0

on learning new things and then we haven't used it. (Gardner and Williamson, 2004:55)

While, as in the case of other countries, teachers were not unsympathetic to some of the reforms proposed by the education department, it was the number of initiatives and the speed at which schools were expected to respond that was regarded as the major problem. Secondary teachers, in particular, felt threatened by attempts to introduce 'integrated' topics and themes into the curriculum, regarding such initiatives as a 'watered-down curriculum', making insufficient use of their specialist knowledge with an accompanying reduction in students' knowledge and skills.

Special concern was expressed about current inclusion policies paralleling our findings from teachers in England. Allied with the feelings of being under prepared to teach children with special needs was the availability of sufficient resources to support such pupils. Two quotations illustrate these concerns, one from a primary teacher with over 20 years' experience:

> While I'm out on duty in the playground I see around me at least twelve children with disabilities. As there are only going to be two classes in this grade next year I foresee several of them in my class. I can't imagine what it will be like...I am not looking forward to feeling totally inadequate and not in control. Shouldn't staff be educated before being confronted with such problems? (Gardner and Williamson, 2004:64)

While another primary teacher in favour of inclusion but on condition that it received proper funding, expressed the following viewpoint:

> Your planning and preparation times are doubled plus the students take up more of the teacher's time in class. There may not be enough room in the classroom for special equipment. You also have to do PD [professional development] out of school time to learn, for example, how to lift a child. There's a lot to learn in special needs and when you're on your own it's lonely. Unless you practice some things regularly you need to be shown again. (Gardner and Williamson, 2004:63)

Most teachers claimed that pupils' behaviour had declined over the previous five-year period. One member of the support staff in a secondary school described an incident where a pupil told him 'to get f..ed' and went on to comment:

> I feel angry, I could hit him....The last five years kids have been pushing the boundaries. I have the feeling I don't want to be here and am I going to snap? The stress and threat of the work environment, feeling threatened going to the canteen. It's not a nice feeling... If things don't work out I'll leave. (Gardner and Williamson, 2004:53)

Teachers used different strategies to cope with the situation. Some made a decision not to take work home in order to enjoy a better family life while recognising that this would limit their chances of promotion. Some made financial sacrifices by going part-time, while others 'milked the system' by taking days off for sickness in order to catch up with marking and preparation. (Gardner and Williamson, 2004:69)

Common concerns, common solutions?

In all four examples workloads are rising and teachers report increasing pressure. Factors cited are various reform agendas (particularly the consequences of inclusion policies), increased accountability procedures, mounting parental expectations and a decline in student behaviour. However, the stress that teachers feel appears not to be a direct consequence of the hours that they now have to work. Rather it arises from feelings of frustration at not being able to find the time to accomplish any of their required duties (particularly teaching) in a manner which leaves them satisfied 'with a good job done'. This is coupled with a sense that policy makers no longer trust teachers' professional judgments so that reform tends to be mandated rather than introduced, as in the past, through extended consultation and the use of extended trials. In this they share a common concern with their English colleagues.

Ingvarson *et al.* (2005) note that comparative research on the working lives of teachers suggests a need to broaden the discourse when analysing the reasons for teachers' satisfaction/dissatisfaction with their occupation. Previously, models of occupational satisfaction tended to concentrate on the job description, defining the work of a teacher and the conditions under which this work was performed. Now, however, there is a clear need to pay more attention to the ways schools (and teachers) interact with wider economic and political forces within society. Thus in most of the reports, key recommendations tend to focus on reducing the influence of these societal factors rather than on the development of more effective teaching strategies. In Canada, Dibbon (2004) called for increases in non-contact time to allow for better liaison with parents and more time on personal-professional development to raise the status of teaching. This time would be found by reducing class sizes, cutting out supervision duties and increasing the allocation of 'free' periods for planning, preparation and marking. Hong Kong recommendations include attempts to raise the status of teachers through the introduction of Chief Executive Awards for Teaching Excellence, enlarged opportunities for outside experts to foster partnerships with schools, greater professional development opportunities designed to help teachers cope with a society 'that is forever changing'. Again, finding time for teachers to engage in these activities comes from increasing non-contact time by reducing supervision duties, reducing teaching loads (or alternatively class sizes) to be decided on a school-by-school basis, and by reducing the impact of reforms by extending the consultation period and carrying out field trials.

In both New Zealand and Tasmania reductions in non-contact time are to enable teachers to extend links to the wider community through appropriate professional development. This additional time is to be created by cutting down on supervision duties and administrative tasks through greater use of ancillary staff. It would seem therefore that the issues of most concern are not uniquely a matter of a particular government policy but have wider global repercussions.

Governments around the world are subject to a continuous stream of data from the OECD, from Eurostat, The European Commission, from comparative research on pupil performance such as TIMSS (The Third International Mathematics and Science Study). Politicians and policy makers take these data extremely seriously because they are linked (allegedly) to economic performance, with schools held accountable for national competitiveness. Nowhere is this seen more clearly than in the US where major government tracts such as *A Nation at Risk* (1983) propels new tests, new curricula, more concentrated focus on those measurable subjects such as Mathematics, all this despite a continuing lack of evidence (Berliner and Biddle, 1998; Nicholls and Berliner, 2005) to support such a connection. In all countries there are alternative options available to them, some without substantial cost, some requiring a higher level of investment or redirection of investment if policy makers are willing to listen to the voice of the profession and the substantive findings both nationally and internationally on teachers' personal and professional lives.

The chapter has identified some of the key factors affecting the working lives of teachers in other countries which may resonate with teachers in English primary, secondary and special schools. As we have argued, workforce remodelling was prompted by mounting evidence of teacher stress and dissatisfaction not only in UK countries but in light of international evidence too. However, to what extent it has addressed the deeper lying issues of purposes, pedagogy and the very nature of schooling in the twenty-first century remains a more contested issue. It is one which we attempt to address in the final chapter.

 ## Questions for discussion

Does it help to view the issues of teachers' work-life balance from an international perspective?

How far are the concerns about new initiatives, which are generally seen as necessary by most teachers, a reaction against change of any kind?

What reactions do you have to the Tasmanian teachers' strategies for coping with overwork?

10

Remodelling: Structures or Mindset?

Has remodelling of the workforce changed structures or fundamentally affected conceptions of who are the teachers? This chapter explores this question. We start with Ruth Kelly's prediction of a teacher's changing role from instructing to managing and wonder if the next decade will in fact be any different from the preceding three in which revolution was always just around the corner.

What will teachers be doing ten years from now?

Writing in the Sunday newspaper, *The Observer*, Mary Riddle (2007) recounts an incident when Gordon Brown, then Chancellor of the Exchequer, was preparing to take over as Prime Minister. He invited the then Education secretary, Ruth Kelly, to hear his vision of education for the twenty-first Century. In the course of the discussion he asked Ms Kelly, 'What will teachers be doing ten years from now?', She is said to have replied, 'They'll be managing learning; not teaching.'

Whether this will be indeed be true in ten years, as technology grows ever more sophisticated and sites for learning move progressively away from the classroom, is a matter for debate. Predictions of a brave new world have been in the ether since the invention of school radio broadcasting, each new technological advance bringing with it the promise of liberating teachers from direct instruction. In the 1960s the transformation of classroom learning, it is was thought, would be realised through educational television, individualised instruction, programmed learning and, among many other new waves in the 1980s and the 1990s, independent learning systems (ILS). With each new technology there have been those who have prophesied a changing role for teachers whereby they become supervisors rather than instructors of pupils' learning. A seminal publication in 1970, Taylor's *The Teacher as Manager* was given to each new staff appointee at a Scottish college of education, preparing staff to reframe the nature of their work with trainees whose role would be radically different in the future.

These initiatives have come and gone without any major change in what teachers do. Nor until now has the shift towards a greater managerial role and the diminution in the value of face-to-face classroom interaction been a part of official policy. Indeed, the publication of OECD comparative data, cherry-picking visits by policy advisers to Taiwan and other Pacific Rim countries, have served to reinforce the didactic role of the teacher and placed a requirement on Ofsted inspectors to observe whole class teaching.

The evidence from our studies is that the remodelling agreement has effected a significant change, less in respect of the *what* and *how* of pedagogy than in the *who* of classroom instruction. While the rhetoric and official guidance has continued to place the role of teachers centre stage, the introduction of PPA time and differential staffing roles now sees teachers, both by default and design, managing learning at a distance. It has been widely accepted that in some instances (in practice it would appear to be the majority), teaching assistants, with a further short training period, are able to stand in front of a class and deliver sections of the curriculum. Most primary schools have chosen to interpret this as referring to lessons other than numeracy or literacy, hence the prevailing practice in primary schools of using afternoons for PPA time when by tradition, these core subjects are rarely timetabled. The different timetabling structures of secondary schools, however, means that there is not the same distinction between mornings and afternoon sessions and unqualified staff can, and do, stand in for teachers who are ill, who are on PPA time or other forms of planned absence. As we have seen, 'cover' may take a variety of forms, from a dedicated group of TAs acting as a reservoir of expertise (see Chapter 8) to ad hoc pragmatic arrangements. While some head teachers will not allow unqualified staff to take a whole class, they also told us that their resistance is likely to be unsustainable in the future as costs of cover become prohibitive and as some unqualified staff demonstrate exceptional inter-personal skills and expertise in supporting pupils' learning.

It is not surprising that workforce remodelling reforms have resulted (according to Stevenson, 2007:239) in the work of teachers 'being fractured both horizontally (with the removal of lower order teaching activities) and vertically (as academic and pastoral roles are artificially divided, with the latter annexed from teachers' work at all levels of responsibility'. Recommendations from the PricewaterhouseCooper study failed to take account of the fact that teachers continually operate at both the cerebral and the emotional level in their decision-making and that teaching is as much about the heart as it is about the head. Every action involves what the eminent social psychologist, Gordon Allport (1966) termed *coping* and *expressive* behaviour. Allport illustrates these concepts by exploring the behaviour of someone in a room when a companion has forgotten to shut the door on leaving, thus causing a draught. The *coping* action is to shut the door to stop the draught. The *expressive* action is to either close the door quietly or slam it depending on the degree of annoyance felt at the companion's thoughtlessness. Putting up displays, doing photocopying, rehearsing the pupils' seven time tables, reading a story, checking absences may all within a time and motion study appear fairly low-level coping activities and tasks replaceable by others, but for teachers any or all of these tasks may carry important expressive overtones. Standing around the photocopier, chatting while waiting one's turn, often provided important 'collegial moments'. As we reported in the primary study (Galton and MacBeath, 2002) putting up displays were times for conversation, sharing and discussion of children's work, evaluation of quality, exchange of expertise and an important source of professional satisfaction.

A common strand within Labour government reforms has been a determined effort to link liberalisation of the curriculum, greater emphasis on creativity, higher-order thinking and formative assessment with the need to extend the standards agenda. Teachers are encouraged to explore new ways of motivating pupils so as to halt the decline in the attitudes to key subjects such as science, mathematics and modern languages. At the same time they are told to maintain continuing pressure on those pupils who are not meeting the required targets at Key Stages 2 and 3. This despite the fact, as is clear from our evidence, strongly supported by the Primary Review's (2007) community soundings, that most teachers attribute the lack of motivation among their pupils to the target-driven regime.

Introducing the government's initiative on personalised learning at the 2004 North of England Education Conference, David Milliband insisted that teachers should have 'high expectations of every child, given practical form by high quality teaching, based on sound knowledge and understanding of every child's needs'. While this formula hardly seems a task for an unqualified member of support staff, one year later there appears a significant caveat. In a 2005 DfES document setting out the ideas behind the personalisation concept, the remodelling agenda endorsed the fragmentation of teaching into higher and lower order teaching roles with the latter increasingly undertaken by classroom assistants while teachers would focus on 'higher-order skills' (Stevenson, 2007: 245). Personalised learning was defined as a system:

> That should focus on the needs of the individual child with intensive small group tuition in literacy and numeracy for those falling behind and extra stretch for the gifted and talented.

No prizes for guessing which of the groups the teacher is expected to work with more often. This 'official view' differs somewhat from the review group, set up by the Department to conduct 'blue skies thinking' about the nature of the curriculum and teaching in the year 2020. The 2020 vision statement (DfES, 2006) sees personalised learning and teaching as 'taking a highly structured and responsive approach to each child and young person's learning' so that personalised learning is 'learner-centred, knowledge-centred and assessment-centred'.

In a recent survey of how schools were attempting to implement personalised learning (Sebba *et al.*, 2007), the most frequently cited initiatives were incorporated within *The Learning to Learn* philosophy (James *et al.*, 2006) and its attendant *Assessment for Learning* framework (Black and Wiliam, 1988; Black *et al.*, 2003). This, coupled with a greater emphasis on 'pupil voice', suggests that rather than becoming a simple 'division of labour' into 'low-' and 'high-'order tasks, teaching will in the future become even more demanding at all levels. Crucial to the Learning to Learn approach is the need to support the pupils' initial attempts to become *metacognitively wise*, using supportive scaffolding that embraces teaching strategies more sophisticated in nature than the usual demonstration or 'guided discovery' (Galton, 2007). The same is true of Assessment for Learning if it is not to be mere tokenism with a range of techniques such as wait, time, no hands up, traffic lights (pupils to post a red signal when they need help and a green one when they don't). The kind of questioning which promotes learning is not a simple matter of applying a period of wait-time but requires what Alexander (2006) has termed 'dialogic teaching', the engagement of young minds in a critical discourse of which their teachers are part, reflecting and inquiring together.

Alexander's experience suggests that even after further training teachers still find it a challenging task to improve their teaching skills to a point where they no longer resort to what has been characterised as *cued elicitations* (Edwards and Mercer, 1987). For Alexander (2006:50), the dilemma is how to achieve the perfect marriage between pedagogical form and content – central to questions of 'what' and 'how' to teach. He quotes Nystrand (1997) that 'the bottom line for learning, what ultimately counts, is *the extent to which instruction requires students to think, not just report someone else's thinking* [author's own italics]. The *what* of instruction, the content and subject matter is, they argue, critical to learning as well as the *how* of instruction – the question/answer sequences evidenced in face-to-face interaction. What then are the chances of even the most skilled HLTAs achieving this level of competence after only several post-school training sessions?

There is another point at issue here with a direct bearing on the work-life balance of the teaching profession. As we showed in the preceding chapter on teacher workloads in four countries, the biggest impact outside actual classroom teaching is the time and energy devoted to planning and assessment. Both the approaches enshrined in Learning to Learn and Assessment for Learning suggest a reduction in the amount of initial planning and subsequent marking of written assessments. First, because planning has in some cases to be a joint activity between the teacher and the pupil and second, because in the process of becoming *metacognitively wise* pupils have to be able to acquire what psychologists term 'executive control'; that is they have to learn to spot their own errors rather than have them pointed out by a teacher in the form of written comments when s/he marks the exercise books.

The more children and young people assume control of their own learning the greater the pedagogic insight and skill it will require of the teachers. The more children and young people become independent and inter-dependent learners the greater the strategic resourcefulness it will imply for those who lead and shape their learning. The more there is a genuine sense of agency among learners the greater the need for an agential capacity on the part of teachers. This does not preclude activities which we generally associate with conventional teaching, such as rapid question and answer sessions, demonstrations and direct instruction, for example. They will still form part of a teacher's pedagogic repertoire although a smaller and complementary part, but one that rests on fine judgement as to when, where and how to intervene in the learning process and to what end.

Clearly, the above scenario does not fit easily with the 'division of labour' approach and the bartering of PPA time out in exchange for having your pupils taught or supervised by unqualified staff. The value of the teaching assistant lies in a form of partnership with the teacher both in the planning and teaching/learning process, coupled with a shared intelligence as to strategies which meet the diverse needs of students, needs which arise spontaneously and unpredictably during the course of the lesson. That is the kind of support that the teachers we interviewed valued most.

None of these concerns appear to worry Ofsted Inspectors. In their evaluation of the implementation of workforce reform they claim that there has been a revolutionary shift in the culture of the school workforce (Ofsted, 2007:21) with over 75 per cent of the teachers in 55 primary and 45 secondary schools reporting that they now have 'more control over their work, had time to plan collaboratively, develop resources, keep up with assessment and liaise with colleagues' (ibid. 15). While agreeing that PPA time has had a major impact, particularly in primary schools, we are less certain of Ofsted's further conclusion that the major consequence of this revolutionary shift has been wholesale improvements in teaching and learning. Whereas, teachers in our study expressed concerns about the effects on pupils' learning as a result of placing TAs in sole charge of classes, the inspectors appear to suggest that teachers in their study had no such reservations. In numerous examples the report cites, approvingly, examples of TAs in primary schools covering for absences and PPA time and where, at secondary level, non-qualified assistants have taken over responsibility for the management of pastoral care and most of the inclusion agenda. The inspectors judge that this wider workforce was deployed effectively in 75 per cent of the schools visited (ibid. 21). Clearly, the inspectorate share Ruth Kelly's twenty-first century vision of teachers as managers of learning while others, less well qualified, 'deliver' under (and sometimes without) teacher supervision.

The viewpoints expressed in the previous chapters suggest that many teachers are not willing to subscribe to this vision. Our sample was much smaller than Ofsted's but we believe it represents the reality of the situation. This is not the first occasion in which Ofsted have reported positively on government initiatives only for subsequent research to reveal that their assessments were over-optimistic. In their evaluation of the first four years of the Literacy strategy (Ofsted, 2002b) for example, Ofsted warmly endorsed the improvements brought about by whole class interactive teaching when delivered at pace. Contrast this judgement with a more recent paper from the Government sponsored Innovations Unit (Cordgingley *et al.*, 2003:4–5) stating that the strategy had resulted 'in a rash of lessons and closing plenaries characterised by fast and furious closed questions and superficial answers rather than exploratory discussion and reviewing learning that was the aim.' This latter conclusion has the support of several research studies (Alexander, 2001; Galton, 2007:24–28; Hardman *et al.*, 2003; Hargreaves *et al.*, 2003).

There are those critics who would argue that such positive endorsements of government policies are a natural consequence of an arrangement whereby Ofsted is dependent for its funding on those responsible for the policy. Others argue, that, arising out of previous negative experiences, teachers tend to tell inspectors what, it is assumed, they wish to hear. Another explanation, however, is that whereas Ofsted inspectors continually emphasise that they only base their judgements on what they see and what they are told, researchers are more likely to probe more deeply and systematically into what is said, and what is meant by what is said and not said. For this reason, researchers place great importance on recording of interviews, on analysis of transcripts, on supplementary questions which attempt to penetrate beyond the surface of an interviewee's response. Subsequent analysis pays close attention to instances that don't fit a pattern as well as those that do. We believe that this has allowed us, in this instance, to produce a richer and more penetrating analysis than that provided by Ofsted (2007), even with our smaller sample.

Coping with pupil behaviour

A noticeable change in the climate of schooling since our earlier surveys has been the extent to which teachers singled out pupil behaviour as a major source of stress and of additional work. In the 2002 primary survey, classroom disruption was not highlighted as a major problem. Five years on, teachers in the same schools regard it as a more significant priority and the language they use to depict the situation is reminiscent of their secondary colleagues. Teachers claimed that pupils, even in the early years of primary education, were reluctant to follow instructions and that a minority could be extremely confrontational, use foul language and could even be physically aggressive. One Year 3, teacher described an incident where a boy picked up his chair and attempted to throw it at her. Fortunately the aim was poor, but the chair hit the interactive white board causing extensive damage. Teachers newer to the profession tended to blame the deterioration in classroom discipline on poor parenting and on the increase in the number of children with serious learning difficulties now entering primary schools as the result of 'inclusion without adequate resourcing'. Longer serving teachers tended to attribute the decline to the pressures emanating from the 'performance culture'.

It is increasingly common for primary schools to adopt discipline policies in which the rules governing conduct are clearly spelt out in classroom displays together with the consequences for breaking them. At secondary level, verbal warnings are followed by after-school detentions, letters home to parents, a period in the school's referral unit and eventually temporary or permanent exclusion. In the case of one small rural primary school (with an intake from mainly affluent middle-class families), loss of playtime during lunch time or morning break replaced after-school detentions. Working under the supervision of the deputy performed a similar function to referral units in secondary schools (Galton, 2007:116). In both cases, the net effect on teachers was the same – supervision of detention during lunchtime and morning breaks, adding to the workload plus an 'incident' report to be completed. Senior management were thus in a position to defend the schools' stance should an irate parent challenge the decision.

In an effort to reduce sanctions and concomitant workload schools are tending to adopt systems of reward for acceptable behaviour. For example, in one primary school a prerequisite number of tokens earns five minutes extra play. In a secondary school a given number of tokens earns a voucher which could then be exchanged either for free snacks or a drink in the school canteen. Pupils could accumulate enough credits to earn a place on a trip or even a day off school!

In the US, Emmer and Aussiker (1989) concluded that such approaches tend to enjoy limited success. In secondary schools revisited, two to three years on, we saw little signs that attempts to revamp discipline policies had led to a marked improvement in pupil behaviour. In an effort to build up the number of credits for pupils with negative attitudes to school, teachers often differentiated their responses to pupils. More difficult pupils would be rewarded for simply listening, or being polite to a classmate, whereas pupils whose behaviour was generally acceptable would have to do something exceptional to earn their credit. In one school the whole of a lower set were given a credit for walking silently in a straight line to assembly- whereas for the top set credit was awarded for collecting a large amount of 'sponsorship money' for a Wildlife Trust. The net result, over time, was to devalue the 'credit currency' since the more able pupils soon saw that the tokens were not worth having.

Yet, as Watkins and Wagner (2000:48) argue, a 'one-size-fits-all' approach does not take sufficient account of differing pupils' backgrounds. An introverted pupil who misbehaves because he wishes to 'keep in with the lads' is a very different case from an able pupil who reacts through boredom, or the child from an abusive family who carries violence experienced at home into the school setting. The embrace of staged and token responses limits the possibility of discussion and negotiation which are not only essential to intelligent differentiation of sanctions but also an essential aspect of the learning process. As most teachers differentiate between rules governing behaviour on the one hand and cognitive development on the other, the message that pupils receive from the very first days of schooling is 'when it's to do with learning do as you [*the pupil*] think, but when it's to do with behaving do as I [*the teacher*] say' (Galton, 1989). Whereas for the teacher this message is an unambiguous one, for pupils the distinction between behaving and learning may be less clear-cut since 'teachers sometimes ask questions to find out if you are paying attention and sometimes to find out what you know'. The system appears not to be designed to involve classroom teachers in an analysis of this kind.

Current initiatives such as *Assessment for Learning* (Black *et al.*, 2003) and *Learning to Learn* (James *et al.*, 2006) share the same perspective – that if pupils are to become autonomous learners they must be able to question the strategies that they use and the decisions they make in attempting to solve intellectual problems. While extreme misbehaviour in the classroom obviously demands a swift, uncompromising response, so that classroom rules are unequivocal, pupils are not often expected to apply the same metacognitive skills that they use for academic problem solving to issues of personal relationships, except perhaps in PSHE and citizenship classes.

These anomalies and inherent contradictions convey powerful subliminal messages. For example, motivation to listen carefully and courteously to the teacher or to fellow pupils rests on a desire to win a free can of cola rather than from a growing understanding of their interdependence and mutual accountability as human beings. This then cuts across attempts to encourage pupils to exercise a voice in relation to behaviour and learning, regarded by the government as an essential component of *Personalised Learning* (Sebba *et al.*, 2007). The idea that pupil themselves have something significant to say about the organisation and conduct of classroom relationships is not a recent creation; its origins can be found in earlier attempts to resolve classroom conflict by creating a classroom climate where *nobody wins and nobody loses* (Gordon, 1974). Gordon quotes one teacher who having participated in one of the training sessions decided to change his approach.

> I was ready to quit teaching because of the constant need to be a disciplinarian. The course showed me that the real problem was my rules – I made them and had to reinforce them – that's all I accomplished most of the time. When I let the class set the rules this changed, I have time to teach now and students liked me more because I am a teacher instead of a disciplinarian. I don't know if they learn any more but we have a lot more fun learning it. (Gordon, 1974:272)

Followers of Gordon's methods find that a surprisingly high proportion of teachers either stay locked into a win-lose approach, where either I [*teacher*] win and you [*pupil*] lose or I [*teacher*] lose and you [*pupil*] win. According to Gordon (1974), mostly teachers vacillated back and forth between the two alternative positions, depending on the mood of the moment and few appeared to be aware of alternatives to win-lose conflict-resolution methods or even that they were in fact employing 'a method'. Most teachers, he contended, 'play it by ear', or 'fly blind'. He found it was rare for teachers to recognize any direct connection between their conflict-resolution methods and the behaviour of their students.

Two decades on from Gordon's research teachers have benefited from a much greater wealth of information, critique and professional development but the question remains as to how much the system itself and prevailing social forces are driving teachers back into the kind of behaviour which Gordon observed.

 Case Study Context: Lining up for learning

Gordon cites the case of a teacher continually frustrated by pupils not lining up in the playground before class. Eventually, his frustration got the better of him, and he demanded to know why it was that they made him waste ten minutes each morning trying to get them into line. They said it was because they had to stand in line waiting for him 'to arrive to escort them to the classroom and then having to march like soldiers'. Together they negotiated a new arrangement whereby 'when the bell rang, they were to walk to the classroom from the playground and I [the teacher] was to walk from the staffroom, and we'd go in'. It is in this teacher's final comment that the key lesson may be found.

> We save ten minutes on the round up and a lot of time that I used to lecture them on lining up and marching quietly.... But the biggest difference is how we feel about each other when we get into the classroom. Everybody used to be mad by the time we'd lined up and marched quietly to the room. Now we go into the classroom feeling good, or at least not mad at each other. That sometimes saves a whole afternoon.

Leading the remodelled school

Whether or not schools are able to cope with the increasing complexity of workforce reform, embedded within a highly prescriptive government agenda, rests to a significant degree on the quality and ingenuity of leadership. We have visited schools in which head teachers and senior management teams worked inventively in the spaces, redeploying staff so as to manage tasks and meet targets, efficiently, economically and within the parameters of government policy. One cannot help but be impressed by the creative pragmatism of school leaders, moving the pieces on the personnel chessboard, juggling the demands and contradictions of those to whom they have to render an account – the DCSF, Oftsed, the Local Authority, School Improvement Partners, Professional Associations, Partner Schools, as well as parents and community agencies implicit in the *Every Child Matters* guidance framework. It was rarely that they would have chosen to be following such a prescriptive path were they not being driven by an external force field but they admitted to being confronted on a daily basis by paradox. Think long term but deliver results now; innovate but avoid mistakes; be flexible but follow the rules; collaborate but compete; delegate but retain control; encourage teamwork but assess individuals; share leadership but carry responsibility as an individual.

School leaders described themselves as caught in a crossfire of prescriptive national policies on the one hand and local expectations and demands on the other. While attempting to be circumspect in reference to children and families and careful to avoid blaming the parents, school staff were clearly struggling with a new order of social and peer group challenges. Reasonable behaviour in school and parental support out of school could not be assumed and the response to punishment and exclusion often resulted in confrontation and, on occasion, verbal or physical assault. In an attempt not to lay blame at parents' doors the discourse was framed in terms of the mediating influence of newspapers, television, the Internet, the drug, alcohol and permissive culture in which many parents have simply lost control of children as they entered the turbulent adolescent years.

Inclusion policies, which were generally endorsed in principle, were, in practice, often simply unsustainable due to inadequate expertise and resourcing, and forms of behaviour which could only be contained by the full-time policing of a teaching assistant, containment in special units or exclusion from school. Our discussions with parents of children with special needs revealed a deep-seated ambivalence. Parents spoke warmly and with gratitude about schools and teachers who went to inordinate lengths to support their children but also blamed a system that failed them at many turns. In particular, transition from primary to secondary school was typically a fraught experience and frequently emanated in exclusion.

Contacting the automated school

Our own efforts to contact secondary schools were salutary. Letters and e-mails often received no response and trial by telephone was a deeply frustrating experience. Schools, along with businesses had entered the automated age of the disembodied call centre. Typically, a caller is greeted with a message such as the following:

> For admission inquiries please press 1, for staff inquires press 2, for staff vacancies press 3, for pupil attendance press 4, for staff absences and PA to the head teacher press 5, for premises-related matters press 6, for catering press 7. For all other inquiries please hold.

In one secondary school which we were particularly keen to return to after a very rich visit two years previously, 21 unreturned and unanswered phone calls followed an unacknowledged letter and e-mail. After dutifully following the button pressing routine on numerous occasions (number 5 being the head teacher's PA) we were continually greeted with the words 'There is no one here to take your call but please leave a message.' After numerous attempts we began to try other avenues and did on occasion speak to a human voice which informed us that 'they are all in a meeting but if you leave a message they will get back to you' and, on another occasion, a suggestion that we sent an e-mail to the head which we did, but without acknowledgement or reply. Finally, after two weeks we were informed by the PA that the head teacher 'does not have a spare moment' and is 'completely bogged down'.

While it may seem cavalier to persist when our overtures were clearly not welcome, an experience of this kind was valuable in giving us an insight into what it might feel like from a parental point of view. Not only was it a time-consuming and frustrating process but it also conveyed a strong subliminal message about the ethos of the school and also the change of head teacher since our previous visit. Ultimately, the admission that the new head teacher was completely 'bogged down' told its own story. In virtually every school we visited, or where we spoke to an apologetic head over the phone, it was clear that head teachers are now working harder, longer hours and within a more complex and demanding environment. However distributed the leadership, the 12-hour day was not uncommon, weekends were rarely free of school-related work and extended school holidays had become a nostalgic memory. As our evidence, together with that of the Teachers Review Body (2006) shows, this is more acute in secondary than in primary schools, although with wide variations in both sectors. The appointment of business managers, administrative staff and the increasing proliferation of job roles had lessened the pressure in one area while increasing it in another. The bidding economy, confederations, the specialist school, the extended school, the *Every Child Matters* agenda and the need to cope with serial innovation are all taking their toll, while the most addicted of heads admitted to revelling in the adrenalin-fuelled rush of keeping 'one step ahead of the game'.

In the final analysis, workforce reform has proved to be something of a palliative for a system on the verge of implosion but has not affected an improvement in work-life balance, most categorically not for head teachers, neither for increasingly put upon teaching assistants and not, it would appear from our sample, for the majority of school staff. Nor, more significantly has it appeared to touch the deepest level of pedagogy or what transactional analysts would describe as adult-child transactions. The very nature of the highly differentiated staffing structure, divorcing pastoral care and pedagogy, and increasing the distance between those who lead and those who follow, has freed teachers from many tiresome tasks but not from a way of thinking about the nature of curriculum 'delivery'. Indeed, lessons appear more than ever to be delivered rather than becoming a genuine dialogic process. In a climate where teachers can download lesson plans from the Net and hand over lesson protocols to TAs there is, as Robin Alexander (2004) complained, 'still no pedagogy'.

It is easy to lay the primary responsibility on the performativity culture with its competitive 'league' tables, its attendant targets and obsession with testing, so that the mythic relationship with the economy has, in Alison Wolf's (2002:254) words 'narrowed – abysmally and progressively – the vision we have of education itself'. Yet, while there is much to be depressed about in the current climate there is equally much to celebrate. Good teachers have always known how to be educationally subversive. They have refused to underestimate their own sense of agency and have been able to perceive the scope for radical change within their own classrooms and within their own schools. They refuse to collude with the victim mentality which relinquishes initiative, self-belief and a sense of agency. They are encouraged supported and empowered by a senior leadership team which understands that schools learn and change from the bottom up.

Writing in an American context about teacher leadership Ann Liebermann's words have an encouraging resonance.

> They [*teachers*] learned to recognize the fear that accompanies sharing practice publicly and came to understand more acutely what underlies the reticence to expose practice one's peers. They developed a wide range of strategies for building community, for drawing expertise from teachers' participating in professional development, for sharing knowledge and for sharing leadership with others. It encouraged them to work collaboratively and to go public with both their successes and their questions. (Liebermann and Freidrich, 2008)

To answer Garden Brown's question 'what will teachers be doing ten years from now?' the survival of the educational system will depend on the mantra of distributed leadership becoming a reality as teachers themselves, collectively, set the agenda and see themselves not only as leaders of children's learning but as contributing to, and learning from, their colleagues. The time afforded to them through a better resourced and intelligently remodelled school week, allowing them time to observe, to research, to read, to reflect, may not only solve the recruitment and retention 'crisis' but also raise standards in a more meaningful sense than that currently espoused by impatient government ministers.

Most teachers accept that the demands of the twenty-first century require that they change their practice. They are happy to accept guidance on the general principles that should govern their teaching. However, once inside the classroom, only teachers have the expertise, borne out of their daily experience, to determine how best to put such principles into practice. The past decade has seen governments in many countries put pressure on teachers to change the way they teach and then to offer various inducements such as salary restructuring, workload reductions and provision of additional support staff. Such improvements to the teachers' pay and conditions are to be welcomed but count for nothing if there is no driving impulse to return to the classroom day-on-day, year after year. What motivates teachers to remain within the profession and to give of their best is the buzz of a 'magic moment'; when the 'penny finally drops', when the pupil's puzzled gaze gives way to a smile of recognition. It is in these 'magic moments' that teaching meets learning. When that meeting of minds becomes an expectation rather than a rare occurrence teaching reaps its own rewards and learning is no longer the servant of token incentives.

Questions for discussion

What, in your opinion, will teachers be doing ten years from now?

Has the remodelling of the workforce effected an improvement in pedagogy, as Ofsted inspectors have claimed?

What steps should be taken to give the teaching profession ownership and control over pedagogy, thereby allowing a much greater degree of professional autonomy?

What scope and latitude do teachers actually have to make a life in teaching a more rewarding and fulfilling one?

References

Ainscow, M. and Muncey, J. (1989) *Meeting Individual Needs*, London: David Fulton.

Alexander, R. (1995) *Versions of Primary Education*, London: Routledge.

Alexander, R.A (2001) *Culture and Pedagogy: International Comparisons in Primary Education*. Malden, MA: Blackwell Publishers.

Alexander, R. (2004) Still no pedagogy? Principle, pragmatism and compliance in primary education, *Cambridge Journal of Education*, 34 (1): 7–33.

Alexander, R. (2006) *Towards Dialogic Teaching: Rethinking Classroom Talk*, 3rd ed., York: Dialogos, UK Ltd.

Allport, G. (1966) Expressive behaviour. In Semeonoff, B. (ed), *Personality Assessment*, London: Penguin Books.

Audit Commission (2002) *Getting in on the Act – Provision for Pupils with Special Educational Needs: The National Picture*, London: HMSO.

Bach, S., Kessler, I. and Heron, P. (2006) Changing job boundaries and workforce reform: the case of teaching assistants, *Industrial Relations Journal*, 37 (1): 1–21.

Baker, K. (1993) *The Turbulent Years: My Life in Politics*, London: Faber and Faber.

Ball, S. (2001) Labour, learning and the economy: a political sociology perspective. In Fielding, M. (ed), *Taking Education Really Seriously: Four Years Hard Labour*, London: RoutledgeFalmer.

Ball, S.J. (2008) *The Education Debate: Policy and Politics in the Twenty-first Century*, London: Routledge.

Bellivieu, G., Liu, X. and Murphy, E. (2002) *Teacher Workload on Prince Edward Island*, Prince Edward Island Teacher's Federation.

Bennett, N. (1976) *Teaching Styles and Pupil Progress*, London: Open Books.

Berliner, D. (2006) Unpublished presentation as discussant as American Research Association Symposium, San Francisco, April 10th.

Berliner, D. and Biddle, B. (1998) *The Manufactured Crisis*, Reading, MA: Perseus Books.

Black, P. and Wiliam, D. (1988) *Inside the Black Box: Raising Standards Through Classroom Assessment*, London: King's College, University of London.

Black, P., Harrison, C., Lee, C., Marshall, B. and Wiliam, D. (2003) *Assessment for Learning: Putting it into Practice*, Maidenhead, UK: Open University Press.

Brehony, K. (2005) Primary schooling under New Labour, *Oxford Review of Education*, 31 (1): 29–46.

Brown, M., Askew, M., Baker, D., Denvir, H. and Millett, A. (1998) Is the National Numeracy Strategy research based? *British Journal of Educational Studies*, 46: 362–385.

Butt, G. and Gunter, H. (2005) Challenging modernisation: remodelling the educational workforce, *Educational Review*, 57 (2): 131–137.

Campbell, J. (1998) Broader thinking about the primary school curriculum, *Take Care, Mr Blunkett*, London: Association of Teachers and Lecturers (ATL).

Campbell, J. and Neill, J. (1994) *Primary Teachers at Work*, London: Routledge.

Carter, S.C. (2001) *No Excuses: Lessons from 21 High-Performing High-Poverty Schools*, New York, NY: Heritage Foundation.

Cordgingley, P., Bell. M., Evans, D. and Firth, A. (2003) *What do Teacher Impact Data Tell Us about Collaborative CPD?* London: DfES/EPPI/CUREE.

Croll, P. and Moses, D. (1985) *One in Five: The Assessment and Incidences of Special Educational Needs*, London: Routledge & Kegan Paul.

CTF (2003) *A National Survey of Teacher Workload and Worklife,* August edition.

d'Arbon, T., Duignan, P., Duncan, D. J. and Goodwin, K. (2001) Planning for the future leadership of Catholic schools in New South Wales. *British Educational Research Association Annual Conference*, University of Leeds, September 13–15.

Davies, M. and Edwards, G. (2001) Will the curriculum caterpillar ever learn to fly? In Fielding, M. (ed), *Taking Education Really Seriously: Four Years Hard Labour*, London: RoutledgeFalmer.

Day, C. (2000) Teachers in the twenty-first century: time to renew the vision, *Teachers and Teaching*, 6 (1): 101–115.

Department for Education and Skills (2006) *Raising Standards and Tackling Workload: A National Agreement*, London: Department for Education and Skills.

Department for Education and Skills (2006) *Raising Standards and Tackling Workload Implementing the National Agreement*, Note 16.

DES (Department of Education and Science) (1978) *Warnock Committee Report*, London: HMSO.

DfE (Department for Education) (1994) *Code of Practice for the Identification and Assessment of Special Educational Needs,* London: Department for Education.

DfES (2003a) *Excellence and Enjoyment: A Strategy for Primary Schools*, London: Department for Education and Skills.

DfES (2003b) *Raising Standards and Tackling Workload: A National Agreement*, London: Department for Education and Skills.

DfES (2004) *Removing the Barriers to Achievement*, London: Department for Education and Skills.

DfES (2005) *Higher Standards, Better Schools for All*, Annesley, Notts: DfES Publications.

DfES (2006) *2020 Vision,* Report of the Teaching and Learning in 2020 Review Group, Annesley, Notts: DfES Publications.

Dibbon, D. (2004) *It's About Time!! A Report on the Impact of Workload on Teachers and Students*, St Johns, NL: Faculty of Education, Memorial University of Newfoundland.

Draper, J. and McMichael, P. (2000) Contextualising new headship, *School Leadership & Management*, 20 (4): 459–473.

Dyson, A. (2004) *Inclusion and Pupil Achievement*, Available at: www.dfes.gov. uk/research Economic and Members Services Bulletin, Canadian Teachers' Federation.

Edwards, D. and Mercer, N. (1987) *Common Knowledge and the Development of Understanding in the Classroom*, London: Routledge.

Eisner, E. (2005) *Reimagining Schools*, London: Routledge.

EMB (2006) *The Report of the Committee on Teachers' Work*, Final Report of the Committee under the Chairmanship of Professor Edmond Ko: Education and Manpower Bureau.

Emmer, E. and Aussiker, A. (1989) School and classroom discipline programs: how well do they work? In Moles, O. (ed), *Strategies to Reduce Student Misbehaviour*, Washington, DC: US Department of Education.

Entwistle, N.J. (1987) *Understanding Classroom Learning*, London: Hodder & Stoughton.

Frean, A. (2007) Less than half of teachers have degree in subject, *The Times*.

Frost, D. (2005) Resisting the Juddgernaut: building capacity through teacher leadership in spite of it all, *Leading and Managing*, 10 (2): 83.

Fujita, H. (1997) *A Study on the Culture of Teaching and Teacher Professionalism in Japan*, Tokyo: University of Tokyo.

Galton, M. (1989) *Teaching in the Primary School*, London: David Fulton.

Galton, M. (1995) *Crisis in the Primary Classroom*, London: David Fulton.

Galton, M. and Fogelman, K. (1998) The use of discretionary time in the primary school, *Research Papers in Education*, 13: 119–139.

Galton, M.(2007) *Learning and Teaching in the Primary Classroom*, London: Sage Publications.

Galton, M. and MacBeath, J. with Charlotte Page and Susan Steward (2002) *A Life in Teaching? The Impact of Change on Primary Teachers' Working Lives*, Faculty of Education, Cambridge: University of Cambridge.

Galton, M., Gray, J. and Rudduck, J. (2003) *Transfer and Transitions in the Middle Years of Schooling (7–14) Continuities and Discontinuities in Learning*, Research Report RR443, Nottingham: DfEE Publications.

Galton, M., Simon, B. and Croll, P. (1980) *Inside the Primary Classroom*, London: Routledge & Kegan Paul.

Gardner, C. and Williamson, J. (2004) *Workloads of government school teachers and allied educators in Tasmania*, a report commissioned by the Australian Education Union (Tasmanian Branch). Launceston: Faculty of Education, University of Tasmania.

General Teaching Council of Wales (2002) *The Teacher Recruitment Survey*, GTCW.

Giles, C. and Dunlop, S. (1989) Changing directions at Tile Hill Wood. In Ainsow, M. and Florek, A. (eds), *Special Educational Needs towards a Whole School Approach*, London: David Fulton.

Gordon, T. (1974) *T.E.T. Teacher Effectiveness Training*, New York, NY: Peter Wyden.

Hardman, F., Smith, F. and Wall, K. (2003) Interactive whole class teaching in the National Literacy Strategy, *Cambridge Journal of Education*, 33 (2): 197–215.

Hargreaves, A. (2005) Video interview: dimensions of leadership. Available at: http://www.nationalpriorities.org.uk/Resources/Miscellaneous/NCSL/index. html:last accessed 20/3/08.

Hargreaves, L., Moyles, J., Merry, R., Patterson, F., Pell, A. and Esarte-Sarries, V. (2003) How do primary school teachers define and implement interactive teaching in the national literacy strategy in England? *Research Papers in Education*, 18 (3): 217–236.

Harvey, A. and Spinney, J. (2000) *Life on the Job: A Time-use Study of Nova Scotia Teachers*, Halifax: Time-use Research Programme, Saint Mary's University.

Hilsum, S. and Cane, M. (1971) *The Teachers' Day*, Slough: NFER.

HMSO (2003) *Education (Specified Work and Registration) England Regulations*, London: Her Majesty's Stationary Office.

Ingersoll, R.M. (2003) *Is There Really a Teacher Shortage?* (Center of the Study of Teaching and Policy). Philadelphia, PA: University of Pennsylvania.

Ingvarson, L., Kleinhenz, E., Beavis, A., Barwick, H., Carthy, I. and Wilkinson, J. (2005) *Secondary Teacher Workload Study Report*, A study commissioned by the Ministry of Education, New Zealand, Hawthorn, Victoria: Australian Council for Educational Research (ACER).

James, C. and Whiting, D. (1998) The career perspectives of deputy head teachers, *Educational Management and Administration*, 26 (4): 353–362.

James, M., Black, P., McCormick, R., Pedder, D. and Wiliam, D. (2006) Learning how to learn in classrooms, schools and networks: aims, design and analysis, *Research Papers in Education,* 21 (2): 101–118.

Johnson, S.M. (2004) *Finders and Keepers: Helping New Teachers Survive and Thrive in Our Schools*, San Francisco, CA: Jossey-Bass.

Kingston, P. (2007) Mr J's big questions, Teaching Awards 2007, *Education Guardian*.

LeBlanc, C. (2000) *The Workloads and Conditions of New Brunswick Teachers*, Fredericton, NB: New Brunswick Teachers' Federation.

Lewis, A. and Norwich, B. (eds) (2005) *Special Teaching for Special Children: Pedagogies for Inclusion*, Maidenhead, UK: Open University Press.

Lieberman, A. and Friedrich, L. (2007) Changing teachers from within: teachers as leaders. In MacBeath, J. and Cheng, Y.C. (eds), *Leadership for Learning: International Perspectives*, Amsterdam: Sense Publishers.

Livingstone, I. (1999) *The Workload of Primary Teaching Principals: A New Zealand Survey*, Wellington: Chartwell Consultants.

MacBeath, J. (1976) *A Question of Schooling*, London: Hodder and Stoughton.

MacBeath, J. (2007) *The Impact of School Self Evaluation and External School Review in Hong Kong*, Hong Kong: Education Manpower Bureau.

MacBeath, J. and Clark, W. (2005) *School Self Evaluation and External School Review: The Impact Study, First Interim Report*, Cambridge: Cambridge Education.

MacBeath, J. and Galton, M. (2004) *A Life in Secondary Teaching?* Faculty of Education, Cambridge: University of Cambridge.

MacBeath, J. (2006) School Inspection and Self-evaluation: Working with the New Relationship, London: RoutledgeFalmer.

MacBeath, J., Gray, J.M., Cullen, J., Frost, D., Steward, S. and Swaffield, S. (2006) *Schools on the Edge: Responding to Challenging Circumstances*, London: Sage Publications.

McLaughlin, C., Florian, L. and Rouse, M. (2005) *Putting Social Care in the Picture: An Election Campaign Briefing*, Cambridge: Faculty of Education, University of Cambridge.

Martin, P. (1997) *The Sickening Mind*, London: Flamingo.

Milliband, D. (2004) *Personalised Learning: Building a New Relationship with Schools*, Speech to the North of England Education Conference, Belfast, January 8.

Moreno, J.M. (2004) *Keynote Address, The 2nd International Summit for Leadership in Education: Integrity and Interdependence*, Boston, MA: Boston College.

Moseley, D., Elliott, J., Gregson, M. and Higgins, S. (2005) Thinking skill frameworks for use in education and training, *British Educational Research Journal*, 31 (3): 367–390.

NAHT (2003) *Policy Paper on Special Schools*, National Association of Head Teachers at www.naht.org.uk.

Naylor, C. and Malcolmson, J. (2001) 'I love teaching but…' A study of the workload of English teachers in BC secondary grades. In Naylor, C., Schaefer, A. and Malcolmson, J. (eds) *Worklife of BC Teachers: A Compilation of BCFT Research Reports on Working and Learning Conditions in 2001*, Vancouver, BC: British Columbia Teachers' Federation.

Naylor, C. and Schaefer, A. (2003) *Worklife of B.C. Teachers: A Compilation of BCTF Research Reports on Working and Learning Conditions in 2001*, Vancouver, BC: British Columbia Teachers' Federation.

Nicholls, S. and Berliner, D. (2005) *The Inevitable Corruption of Indicators and Educators through High Stakes Testing*, Education Policy Research Unit (EPSL-0503-101-EPRU) Tempe, AZ: Arizona State University.

Normore, A. (2004) Recruitment and selection: meeting the leadership shortage in one large Canadian school district, *Canadian Journal of Educational Administration and Policy*, 30.

NUT (2003) *Special Educational Needs Co-ordinators and the Revised Code of Practice: An NUT Survey*, London: National Union of Teachers.

NUT (2006) *National Union of Teachers Policy Statement on Meeting the Needs of Pupils with Special Educational Needs*, London: National Union of Teachers.

Nystrand, M. (1997) *Opening Dialogue*, New York, NY: Teachers College Press.

OECD (2001) *Teacher Exodus – The Meltdown Scenario*, Paris: OECD Education.

Ofsted (1996) *The Implementation of the Code of Practice for Pupils with Special Educational Needs*, London: Office for Standards in Education.

Ofsted (2002a) *The Curriculum in Successful Primary Schools*, London: Office for Standards in Education.

Ofsted (2002b) *The National Literacy Strategy: The First Four Years, 1998–2002*, London: Office for Standards in Education.

Ofsted (2004) *Special Educational Needs and Disability: Towards Inclusive Schools*, London: Office for Standards in Education.

Ofsted (2005) *Managing Pupil Behaviour*, London: Office of Standards in Education.

Ofsted (2007) *Reforming and Developing the School Workforce*, London: Office for Standards in Education.

OME (2006) *Teachers' Workload Diary Survey*, London: Office of Manpower and Economics.

O'Neill, N. (2002) *A Question of Trust*, Cambridge: Cambridge University Press.

Portin, B. (2004) Learning Opportunities of School Leaders Across National Boundaries: Lessons from an International Collaboration of Schools, Paper presented at the University Council for Educational Administration Annual Conference, Kansas City, Missouri, 12th–14th November.

Primary Review (2007) *Community Soundings: The Primary Review Regional Witness Sessions,* Cambridge: Univesrsity of Cambridge Faculty of Education.

PWC (2001) *Teacher Workload Study,* A Report of a review commissioned by the Department for Education and Skills, London: PricewaterhouseCooper.

Reynolds, D. and Farrell, S. (1996) *Worlds Apart? A Review of International Surveys of Achievement Involving England,* London: HMSO.

Riddle, M. (2007) Be brave, Mr Brown, in the classroom, *The Observer.*

Sachs, J. (2003) Teacher professional standards: controlling or developing teaching? *Teachers & Teaching: Theory and Practice,* 9 (2): 175–186.

Sebba, J., Brown, N., Steward, S., Galton, M. and James, M. (2007) *An Investigation of Personalised Learning Approaches Used by Schools,* Research Report 843, Annesley, Notts: Department for Education and Skills (DfES).

Selwood, I. and Pilkington, R. (2005) Teacher workload: Using ICT to release time to teach, *Educational Review,* 57 (2): 163–174.

Shimahara, N. (2003) *Teaching in Japan: A Cultural Perspective,* New York, NY: Routledge.

Smith, M.K. (2005) Background to the green paper for youth 2005, *The Encyclopaedia of Informal Education,* Available at: www.infed.org/youth work/green_paper.htm. First published; March 20, 2005; Last accessed June 23rd 2007.

Stevenson, H. (2007) Restructuring teachers' work and trade union responses in England: bargaining for change? *American Educational Research Journal,* 44 (2): 224–251.

Surowiecki, J. (2004) *The Wisdom of Crowds,* New York, NY: Random House.

Taylor, G. (1970) *Teacher as Manager,* London: Councils and Educational Press.

Tennant, C. (2001) Work-related stress and depressive disorders, *Journal of Psychosomatic Research,* 51: 697–704.

Thomas, H., Butt, G., Fielding, A., Foster, J., Gunter, H., Lance, A., Pilkington, R., Potts, L., Powers, S., Rayner, S., Rutherford, D., Selwood, I. and Szwed, C. (2004) *The Evaluation of Transforming the School Workforce Pathfinder Project,* Research Report RR541, Annesley, Notts: Department for Education and Skills (DfES).

Thomson, P., Blackmore, J., Sachs, J. and Tregenza, K. (2003) High stakes principalship – sleepless nights, heart attacks and sudden death accountabilities: reading media representations of the United States principal shortage. *Australian Journal of Education,* 47 (2): 118–132.

Tomlinson, S. (2005) *Education in a Post-welfare Society,* 2nd ed., Maidenhead, UK: Open University Press.

Troen, V. and Coles, K. (2004) *Who's Teaching Your Children? Why the Teacher Crisis is Worse than You Think and what can be done about it,* New Haven, CT: Yale University Press.

Tucker, M. and Codding, J. (eds) (2002) *The Principal Challenge: Leading and Managing Schools in an Era of Accountabilities,* San Francisco, CA: Jossey-Bass.

Warnock, M. (2005) *Special Educational Needs: a New Look,* Impact No 11, London: Philosophy of Education Society of Great Britain.

Watkins, C. and Wagner, P. (2000) *Improving School Behaviour,* London: Paul Chapman.

Wedell, K. (2005) Dilemmas in the quest for inclusion, *British Journal of Special Education*, 32 (1): 3–11.

Wilhelm, K., Dewhurst-Savellis, J., Parker, G. (2000) *Teacher Stress? An Analysis of Why Teachers Leave and Why They Stay*, Sidney, NSW, Australia: School of Psychiatry, University of New South Wales.

Williams, T.R. (2001) *Unrecognised Exodus, Unaccepted Accountability: The Looming Shortage of Principals and Vice-Principals in Ontario Public School Boards*, Ontario: School of Policy Studies.

Wolf, A. (2002) *Does Education Matter? Myths about Education and Economic Growth*, London: Penguin Books.

Woods, P., Jeffery, B., Thomas, G. and Boyle, M. (1997) *Restructuring Schools, Reconstructing Teachers*, Buckingham: Open University Press.

Wrigley, T. (2003) *Schools of Hope: A New Agenda for School Improvement*, Stoke-on-Trent: Trentham Books.

Index

page references followed by f indicate an illustrative figure; t indicates a table

Aborigines, 94
accountability, 5–6, 20
    bureaucracy and, 9–10
administrative and clerical tasks, 9, 25, 27,
        32, 40, 42, 82, 88, 91–2, 99t,
        100t, 102–3
    TAs 24 tasks, 85–6
Ainscow and Muncey, 58
Alexander, R.
    1995, 14, 15, 62
    2001, 109
    2004, 17, 114
    2006, 107
Allport, G., 105–6
Asperger's syndrome, 71, 77
Assessment for Learning framework,
        107, 111
attention deficit hyperactivity disorder
        (ADHD), 58, 77
Audit Commission (2002), 58, 60
Australia, 6, 21, 92, 94, 98
    leaving the profession, 7–8
    reluctance to become head teachers,
        10, 12
    see also Tasmania
Australian Council of Educational
        Research (ACER), 99
autism, 71, 73, 84

Baker, K., 35, 78
Ball, S., 15
behaviour of pupils, 11, 37–8, 46–7,
        46t, 51, 53–4, 60, 109–12, 113
    borderline cases, special needs,
        73–4
    changing schools, 75–6, 113
    class policeman, case study, 69
    concentration, lack of, case study, 74
    eager to please, case study, 77
    Isolation Units, 68
    lining up problem, case study, 112

    picking up social clues, case study, 72
    rewards for good behaviour, 110, 111
Bennett, N., 14
Bentley, 18
Berliner, D., 61
Berliner and Biddle, 103
Billivieu *et al.*, 94–5
Black and William, 107
Black *et al.*, 107, 111
Blunkett, D., 16–17, 18, 81
Brehony, K., 17, 18
Brown, G., 104, 115
Brown *et al.*, 17
Bulgaria, 11
burnout, 2, 6
Butt and Gunter, 82, 91

Callaghan, J., 14
Campbell, J., 17
Campbell and Neill, 15, 16, 34t
Canada, 8, 21, 93–5, 96, 102–3
    time spent out of school on various
        activities, 95t
Canadian Teachers Federation (CTF),
        94, 95
Chief Executive Awards for Teaching
        Excellence, Hong Kong, 102
citizenship classes, 50, 111
Clark, C., 81
Clinton, B., 17
Code of Practice 1994, 58
confidence, loss of, 25
contacting schools, 113–16
containment, 68, 69, 113
Continuing Professional Development
        (CPD), 21, 45, 55, 78–9
control, teachers' control of their work, 9,
        14, 29–30, 39, 63, 108
Cordgingley *et al.*, 109
creativity and spontaneity, loss of, 8, 18,
        27–8, 30, 31, 55

cross curricular activities, 14, 39, 43, 49–50
curriculum, history of changes to, 13–19
  change to skills based approach, 35–6
curriculum, overloaded, 2004 survey, 46t, 48–50, 49f
Curriculum Development Institute (CDI), Hong Kong, 96

d'Arbon *et al.*, 10, 12
Davies and Edwards, 18
Day, C., 6
Dearing
  1993 review of National Curriculum, 15
  1994 recommendations, 18
delivery, use of term, 5, 55, 91
DEMOS, 18
Dibbon, C., 95, 102
disciplinary issues *see* behaviour of pupils
'*discretionary/non-discretionary*' teaching time, 15–16
Down's syndrome, 77
Draper and McMichael, 9
dyslexia, 58
Dyson, A., 64

Education Act 1981, 57, 58
Educational Action Zones, 17
Education and Manpower Bureau (EMB) 2006 survey, Hong Kong, 96, 97, 98
Edwards and Mercer, 107
Eisner, E., 63
11-plus, 14
Emmer and Aussiker, 110
English, 16, 17, 52
English as a second language, 59
Entwistle, N.J., 61
ethnicity and exclusion, 60
Every Child Matters, 112, 114
Excellence and enjoyment: A strategy for primary schools, 35
Excellence in Cities, 17
Excellence in Schools, 17
exclusion, 60, 67, 68, 71, 113
expertise, lack of specialist, 78–9
external school review, (ESR), 97

Feinberg, M., 6
flexibility, 26, 28
Foucault, M., 7
Foundation Stage, 41

Frost, D., 8
Fujita, H., 7

Galton, M. (1989), 111
Galton, M. (1995), 35
Galton, M. (2007), 107, 109, 110
Galton and Fogelman, 15, 16
Galton and MacBeath (*A Life in Teaching?*), 7, 13, 32, 34t, 35–6, 39, 40, 41, 42, 43, 106
Galton *et al.* (1980), 14
Galton *et al.* (2002), 62
Galton *et al.* (2003), 45
Gardner and Williamson, 101, 102
General Teaching Council in Wales (GTCW), 7
Gordon, T., 111–12

Hardman *et al.*, 109
Hargreaves, A., 8
Hargreaves *et al.*, 109
Harvey and Spinney, 94
head teachers *see* leadership
health problems, 27
Hilsum and Cane, 14, 23, 34t
Hong Kong, 21, 95–8, 100, 102–3
  accountability, 10
  intensification, 6, 7
  workload, 2, 96–7
hours of work, 24, 28–9, 33–5, 34t, 42, 48, 53, 82, 94, 95t, 96–7, 99t, 100t, 114

Impact Report to the Education Bureau (2007), 97, 98
inclusion, 12, 40, 43, 46t, 47, 57–80, 88, 108, 113
  Tasmania, 101
  success of inclusion, 79–80
  summary of problems, 67–8
Inclusion and Autism: is it working?, 71
independent learning systems (ILS), 104
Information and Communications Technology (ICT), 20, 35, 50, 82, 86
Ingersoll, R.M., 7
Ingvarson *et al.*, 99, 102
initial teacher education, 45
'integrationist' approach to special needs education, problems with, 59–60
intensification, 2, 6–7, 11, 23, 95, 100
Interim Primary Committee, 35
Isolation Units, 68

James and Whiting, 10
James *et al.*, 107, 111

Japan, intensification, 6–7
job satisfaction, 4–8, 16, 50, 54–5, 102, 105–6, 115
  see also work/life balance
Johnson, S.M., 8

Kelly, R., 104
Key Stage 1, 35, 76
Key Sage 2, 9, 35, 41, 84, 106
Key Stage 3, 44–5, 49t, 106
Key Stage tests, 15–16, 62, 98

leadership, 8–9, 20–1, 40, 41, 53, 55–6, 87, 89, 115
  'burden of headship', 10, 114
  remodelled school and quality of leadership, 112–13
  salary, 12
Leading Edge schools, 17
Learning for Life – Learning through Life, 96
Learning Managers, 88
learning support assistants (LSAs), 30, 69–70, 73, 78, 79
  see also teaching assistants
Learning Support Units, 68
Learning to Learn philosophy, 107, 111
LeBlanc, C., 94
Leithwood, K., 8
Lewis and Norwich, 62
Libby, 61
Liebermann, A., 115
Lightfoot, L., 16
listening to children, 26
literacy, 15, 17, 23, 27, 28, 30, 35, 36, 50, 106, 109
  coordinator, 36
  literacy hour, 17, 30
  planning, 33
Livingstone, I., 10
lower ability groups, 83–4

MacBeath, J. (2006), 53, 54
MacBeath, J. (2007), 97
MacBeath and Clark, 7, 10, 97
MacBeath and Galton, 7, 43
MacBeath *et al.*
  2001, 18
  2006, 11, 19
McLaughlin *et al.*, 68
managers, teachers as, 104–5
  headteachers, 55–6
marking, comparison between Hong Kong and England, 97

Martin, P., 9
mathematics, 9, 16, 17, 96, 103, 106
mentoring, 36, 45, 50, 54, 87
metacognitively wise, 107
Milliband, D., 106
mixed ability teaching, 14, 18, 93, 95
modern languages, 106
Morris, E., 81
Mortimer, P., 9
music, 35

Nation at Risk, A, 103
National Agreement for remodelling workforce (2003) *see* remodelling process
National Autistic Society (NAS), 71
National College for School Leadership (NCSL) publications, 56
National Curriculum, 9, 15, 35–6, 44, 58, 79
National Curriculum Council, 15
National Foundation of Educational Research (NFER), 14
National Grid for Learning, 17
National Union of Teachers (NUT), 21, 57, 60, 63
Naylor and Malcolmson, 94
Naylor and Schaefer, 94
'New Deal', 17
New Labour, 16, 18, 106
New Relationship with Schools (Ofsted), 54
New York City school, example of intensification, 6
New Zealand, 6, 98–100, 102–3
  accountability, 10
  workload, 98–100, 99t
newly qualified teachers (NQTs), 30, 36, 44, 51
Nicholls and Berliner, 103
non-contact time, 24–5, 32, 34, 40, 82, 95t, 102–3
Normore, A., 11
numeracy, 15, 17, 23, 27, 28, 30, 35, 36, 50, 106, 109
Numeracy Taskforce, 17
Nystrand, M., 107

Observer, The, 104
OECD (Organisation for Economic Cooperation and Development), 4, 7, 96, 103, 105
Ofsted, 9, 15, 17, 21, 45, 54–5, 98, 105, 108–9
  on special needs, 58, 59, 60, 70

OME (Office of Manpower and
    Economics) *see* Teachers Workload
    Survey
O'Neill, N., 5

Pacific Rim, 105
parents, 77–8, 79, 113
    primary schools, 34t, 35, 37–8
    secondary schools, 46t, 47–8, 54
pastoral managers, 53–4, 108
performance, monitoring, 5, 50, 91, 109
    see also tables, performance
personalised learning, 61, 106–7, 111
Portin, B., 9
Post Primary Teacher Association,
    New Zealand, 99
PPA time (planning, preparation and
    assessment), 88, 89, 107–8
    primary schools, 33, 34–5, 34t, 38–42,
        82–4, 105, 108
    secondary schools, 52, 88, 105
PricewaterhouseCooper, 2001 report, 1,
    19–21, 23, 63, 81, 92, 105
    Canadian experience, 94, 95
primary curriculum, 1960s and
    1970s, 14
primary curriculum, 1990s, 15–16,
    17, 35
primary schools, Hong Kong, 96, 97
primary schools, New Zealand, 98, 99
primary schools, Tasmania, 100, 101
primary teachers' work/life balance,
    23–31
primary teaching workforce,
    remodelling, 32–42, 82–7
    table of types of contract, 90t
    typical day, 33, 34–5
Primary Review (2007), 5, 106
Progress Managers, 87–8
PSHE, 111
Pupil Services Centres, 68
Putman, Lord, 5

Qualifications and Curriculum Authority
    (QCA), 18, 36

recruitment and retention crisis, 7–8,
    19, 51
    examples of teachers leaving profession,
        26–8, 51–2
remodelling process, 81–92, 104–16
    division of labour, 89–92, 90t
    future of teaching, 104–9, 115
    success of remodelling, 88–9, 114–15

see also primary teaching workforce,
    remodelling; secondary school
    surveys
    2004 and 2007
resources, lack of, 28
Riddle, M., 104

Sachs, J., 92
salaries, 12, 14, 42, 91, 115
SATs, 27, 28, 70
school self evaluation (SSE), 97
School Standards and Frameworks Bill, 17
School Teachers' Review Body, 14
science, 27, 96, 103, 106
SEAL (Social and Emotional Aspects of
    Learning), 39
Sebba *et al.*, 107, 111
Seclusion Units, 68
secondary curriculum, 1990s, 18–19
secondary school remodelling, 82, 87–9
    restructuring of roles, 87
    table of types of contract, 90t
    see also secondary school surveys 2004
        and 2007
secondary school surveys 2004 and 2007,
    43–56
    2004, 43–52
    2007, 52–6
    cost of raising standards, 44–5
    obstacles to teaching, 45–6, 46t
    typical day, 48, 52–3
secondary schools, Hong Kong, 96, 97
secondary schools, New Zealand, 99t
secondary schools, Tasmania, 100, 101
SEF (self evaluation form), 53
Selwood and Pilkington, 82
Shimahara, N., 6
Singapore, 6
Smith, J., 81
Smith, M.K., 91
social life, loss of, 25, 27, 29
Social Partnership, 92
societal factors, 11, 78, 102
special needs, 9, 11, 38, 41, 51, 57–80,
    83–4, 87
    aspirational classroom practice, 62
    balance of teachers' work, 71–2
    borderline cases, 72–4
    'integrationist' approach, problems
        with, 59–60
    lack of control over policy, 63
    lack of professional support for
        SENCOs, 60
    problem of grading, 61

special needs (*Cont'd*)
    sample used for study of special needs, 64–5
    Tasmania, 101
    transition to secondary school, 75–6
Special Needs and Disability Act 2002, 62
specialist schools, re-designation, 53
Standard and Effectiveness Unit, 17
Standards Managers, 87–8
'statementing' pupils, 60
Stevenson, H., 81, 91–2, 105, 106–7
Strategic Facility, 73
stress, 1, 8–9, 20, 29
    burnout 2, 6
    Canada, 95
    Hong Kong, 97–8
    New Zealand, 100
    student teachers, 36
Summer Literacy Schools Initiative, 17
support for teaching, 5, 50–2, 60, 81–2, 87–8, 103, 115
    categories of support staff, 90t
    see also learning support assistants; teaching assistants
Sure Start, 17
Surowiecki, J., 8

tables, performance, 4, 5, 15–16, 21, 58, 70, 114
Taiwan, 105
targets, 4, 9, 17, 18, 27, 36, 42, 43, 46t, 47, 57, 61, 68, 76, 88, 91, 95, 106, 112, 114
Tasmania, 98, 100–2, 102–3
    workload, 100t
Teacher as Manager, The (Taylor), 105
Teacher's Day, The (Hilsum and Crane), 14
Teachers' Pay and Conditions Act (1987), 15
Teachers Review Body (2006) *see* Teachers Workload Survey
Teachers Workload Survey (OME 2006), 34t, 35, 53, 82, 114
teaching assistants (TAs), 32, 35, 38, 40–1, 54, 68, 69–70, 71, 82–92, 105, 108, 113
    hierarchy of status, 87
    higher level teaching assistants (HLTAs), 41, 54, 82, 83, 84–5, 87, 107
    insecurity, 85
    24 tasks, 85–6
    workload, 84–6, 114
    see also learning support assistants

Tennant, C., 7
testing, 4, 5, 6, 9, 15, 16, 19, 39, 43, 45, 57, 61, 62, 68, 71, 82, 103, 114
    Hong Kong, 96, 97
Thatcher, M., 14–15, 78
Third International Mathematics and Science Study (TIMSS), 96, 103
Thomas *et al.*, 82
Thomson *et al.*, 8
Tomlinson, S., 17, 58
Tourette's syndrome, 73
Transforming the School Workforce Pathfinder Projects, 82
transition to secondary school, 75–6, 113
Troen and Coles, 7
trust, 13, 20, 98, 102
Tucker and Codding, 10

Ukraine, 11
United Nations Declaration of Human Rights, 62
USA, 6, 8, 17, 103, 115
    accountability, 9, 10
    special needs, 61
    use of tokens for good behaviour, 110

Warnock, Baroness
    1978 Report, 57, 59–60
    2005, 61
Warwick University (2002), 92
Watkins and Wagner, 110
Wedell, K., 59
Wilhelm *et al.*, 7–8
Williams, T.R., 8
Wilson, H., 14
Wolf, A., 114
Woodhead, C., 17, 18
Woods *et al.*, 15, 16
work/life balance, 10, 23–31, 32, 87, 88, 99, 101–2, 107, 114
workload, 12, 13–22, 32, 34t, 35, 38–40, 53, 115
    Canada, 94–5
    constructing a future agenda, 21–2
    New Zealand, 98–100, 99t
    PricewaterhouseCooper 2001 report, 19–21, 81, 92
    Tasmania, 100t
    teaching assistants, 84–6, 114
    see also hours; remodelling process
World Bank report (2004), 11
Wrigley, T., 18–19